THE INVESTOR / LANDLORD'S PROPERTY REFURBISHMENT GUIDE

How to successfully manage a residential property refurbishment project

Georgina Hornsby

If you are already "in property" or just getting started and want to make money letting out your property or by getting the best price for it when you sell it on, you are likely to be involved in some sort of ***property refurbishment****. If you want to start saving time and money when undertaking UK residential property refurbishment projects, want to sleep peacefully and be your own boss, then I'd love to share my tips for managing successful property refurbishments and your own property journey. Read on….*

ISBN 978-1-9998178-0-0

First published by DavisHornsby May 2018.

Email gina@davishornsby.co.uk

Disclaimer

Acknowledgements

Thanks to my husband, Barry, who has given me the time and space to share some of the lessons I have learned through my property investment and project management career.

Thanks to those people who didn't believe in me; without you I may never have become stubborn enough to write this book.

Thanks to Secret Millionaire, Gill Fielding, for inspiring me not only with her classy shoes, but for helping educate me through her stories and training, then becoming my role model.

Thanks to Kevin Green, for firing my imagination with his golden chair and down to earth property investment example.

Thanks, also, to my fellow property investor, Elaina, for her time, constructive writing suggestions and moral support in pulling this guide together.

My thanks to all the wonderful fellow investor landlords I have met over the years and the tenants who have put me to the test and helped me grow.

Thanks to the people at The Book Publishing Academy who have facilitated my getting this book to print.

Thank you for buying this book. I trust you will find the content both informative and interesting and that you manage your next property refurbishment, without sleepless nights, on time, within budget and to the high standard you set yourself.

CONTENTS

PREFACE

Whether you are a seasoned property investor, an accidental landlord, starting out on your first project or just wanting to improve a property to get the best return on your investment, the probability is that you will be involved in refurbishment in one way or other. Whether it is installing a new kitchen, or a new bathroom or carrying out a full programme of refurbishment or conversion of a property into flats or rooms to let, one common fact is that someone is going to have to manage your project. That may be why you decided to read this guide. It will save you a few headaches and restless sleep, worrying about how your project is going. That is, provided you are willing to learn from my experience and mistakes. Using the hints and tips you will find in this guide will help keep you on top of your project.

You are not reading an academic text book. You are reading about what I use as a process to manage my refurbishments. I have honed this framework along the way, making mistakes as I went, some more bizarre than others.

MOST INVESTOR LANDLORDS

The vast majority of UK property investors (some 80% according to Landlord Action 2018) have only one or two properties. That's how I started out, probably just like you. Since then I've lost count of how many times I've refurbished a property to provide a decent home for decent people. Some investors have dozens of properties and may well chose to hire a property project manager. Many of you are, however, likely to have to manage the refurbishment yourself.

WHAT PEOPLE KEPT ASKING

When I started attending property meetings, I met all sorts of people involved in or wanting to learn more before stepping into investing in a property and refurbishment. Trouble was, quite often they found it hard to estimate how much they were going to spend, struggled to be able to say when the property might be ready to market and had all manner of issues during the project. I found people coming up to me and asking questions about how I could predict when my projects would finish, how much things might cost and how to organise the work so that different trades-people didn't keep falling over one another. The same questions came up over and over again, so I decided to write this basic guide to help investor / landlords manage the process using the acronym, PUMA, which I use to help me remember what to do next. If you are having sleepless nights, stop worrying. Refurbishing a residential property need not be too stressful at all. That is, provided you follow a process.

Some of us even enjoy refurbishing residential property and falling in love with the end result. I know I do. Would you agree that it is better to take advantage of the experience of those of us who have already done up / refurbished a few properties and already learned from our mistakes, than to start out alone? After all, we are all only human. You need a tried and tested process which is simple to learn.

INHERITED A PROPERTY?

Maybe you have inherited a property or are looking after it when the more elderly owner goes into residential care. You may need to rent it out or perhaps sell it. Maybe you just don't know where to start. Do you find yourself frequently changing your mind in case there is a better way? There are advantages to holding on to the property, such as no conveyancer's legal fees for selling, no stamp duty, no agents' fees for advertising to sell and no tax if you do sell. Refurbishment may well be the best way to get good tenants and the best rent, but perhaps you have never tackled such a project before. Maybe this is why you are reading this. I will guide you step by step through the fundamental process of managing (supervising if you prefer) a residential property refurbishment.

WHY?

Do you actually know why you want to, or need to refurbish any property? For me, I simply wanted to make sufficient money to fund my retirement and you can too, by taking the right run-down house or flat, in the best street you can afford, refurbishing it and selling it on or renting it out. Wanting more money is seldom a good reason in itself. Personally I did not want to be a burden on the State, living off benefits, in my old age, nor did I want to be unable to pay for my own health care or social care in later life. Being financially free to be able to look after myself, perhaps a cliché, was my motivation.

Let's face it, in the UK, along with other countries, there is growing financial pressure on our health and social care systems, as well as an ageing population. Do we want our children to be paying absurdly high taxes to fund our care? What if you had to make a choice between giving lovely birthday presents and getting your own teeth fixed? Do you want to reach retirement unable to look after yourself financially? I very much doubt it.

You are now reading about a simplified property refurbishment management process, which I have settled upon (making mistakes along the way), through my work experiences and my own property journey.

By the time you get to the end of this guide, you will have the fundamental knowledge to successfully manage a property refurbishment project for yourself. You will have a framework made up of four stages, each of which has no more than five discrete steps, for your project. You will be a position to confidently approach your own project/s once we have looked in some detail at the following:

- How to develop an effective plan
- How to get estimates / quotes and prepare a budget
- How to get the sequence of tasks right
- How to get trades-people involved in your project

- How to monitor how the project is progressing
- How to analyse what is happening on the ground

You may even have a chuckle or two. You will have started to get to know me a little and will have increased your chances of completing your projects on budget, on time and with far fewer headaches than if our paths had never crossed.

Property remains, in my opinion, more or less the number one way of growing your wealth. Anyone "in property" will face having to refurbish something one day. At the outset you may decide not to hand it all over to someone else to do; if so you need something to guide you through the process. Managing a simple project first can be the best way of understanding what someone else should be doing, in the event you hand work over to someone else in the future.

In this guide I aim to help you by steering you through the simplified process I have developed and which I am still using. It has evolved by looking at some of the best (and eliminating the over-kill) of what I have learned about project management throughout the past 20 plus years, in managing various projects and in the UK property market.

There are several excellent property investment books out there, but I've not yet found one which focusses on the management of your property refurbishment. This guide adds to all the other skills you will need as an investor / landlord.

CHAPTER 1 WHAT COULD GO WRONG?

Perhaps you have invested in a property and know what you want to do to improve it, but you don't know how to get a decent price on materials and are unsure how to get going. It might be that you have done a few refurbishments in the past and hit a number of snags. Things can and do go wrong and maybe you wish you knew how to approach things so as to hit fewer snags or deal with them better when they do crop up.

I recall my first flat pack kitchen attempt with horror. Lesson learned? Stick with what you are good at, or as Charles Handy would say "stick with the knitting".

Then there was the day when excavation hit an unexpected old Victorian drain; that delayed the project by several days whilst waiting for the council inspector to come and take a look.

That unexpected drain that caused delays.

Perhaps you, like me, have wished you could have avoided such an inconveniences. The most common things that tend not to go according to plan relate to time and money. I like to think of these under four headings:

- Initial funding
- Not knowing how much money you need and when
- Your precious time
- Trades-people's time

INITIAL FUNDING

You may have refurbished a property trying to do everything yourself, in order to save money as many people do when first starting out, only to find it has taken far longer than you ever imagined. If you have borrowed money, be it a bridging loan, mortgage or investment from a joint venture partner (that might be your parents, friends or another investor) that extra time could upset previously good relationships, couldn't it? Even if it is your own borrowing, you, like many other people, may have only set aside enough to make, say, three repayments only to find that four or five repayments are due before you have a tenant in place or a buyer ready to go.

It is all too easy to set aside that initial funding and find you have run out. The project may well stack up and once the project is sold or you have a tenant in place, you should have the money in the bank. However, you need sufficient money at the outset. Underestimating the amount of initial funding required is a short term problem but can be very painful. Resorting to credit cards is a recipe for even more problems.

RUNNING OUT OF MONEY DURING THE PROJECT

Not knowing how much money you need, or when you are going to need it, is even worse than not having enough money to get started. Maybe you have done up a property before, did not know what it was really going to cost and found you ran out of money, not just that initial funding we have just talked about.

Would you agree you have 3 main choices? You could do less than you had hoped, go for a somewhat more basic standard of finish, or find more money (possibly from someone else) to complete the refurbishment. Consider how hard it is going to be if you don't know how much money you need to do all the work you want to do or *when* you are going to need it. If you borrow money, perhaps from your parents, another investor, crowd funding or a bank, I suspect it may not go down too well if you have had to go back cap in hand and ask for more money when they least expect it. This can make you appear less credible or reliable. Would you agree it might be difficult, if not impossible, to borrow funds from the same people for your next project? Think about it.

Suppose your project is expected to take 18 months. What is the point (even if you do have an accurate estimate of costs) of having all that money on which you are paying interest, sitting in your (low or non-existent interest earning) bank account for a year when you only need some of it for the last few months?

Perhaps you have made one of these mistakes, overspent on some part of the refurbishment early on and run out too soon. How are you supposed to know when you need the next tranche of cash and how much? You will soon find out when we look at how to plan your project budget.

YOUR PRECIOUS TIME

Most people would agree you can't be good at everything. I think you might see how it could be more effective and take less time if you had a bit of a helping hand from the right people? We each only have the same discrete amount of time and no-one can be in more than one place at once. Why be late for your child's school play (or that important hot date) just because you have taken on too much yourself.

Me taking on, perhaps, too much myself.

Why be fretting at property A, because the new double glazing units have not been delivered on time, while you sweat about getting to property B, in order to show someone around? Why put yourself through this, when a bit of practical project management could help you avoid most of that? *Your* time is a precious resource. We each only have 24 hours in each day, whoever you are. No-one really knows how many days we each have, so make the most of your precious time, doing what you are good at and what you enjoy.

TRADES-PEOPLE'S TIME

Maybe you've already had a number of time challenges. We've all come across such issues at some time. Perhaps the electrician you hired has been standing around waiting for the tiler to finish his work and get out the way. Time is money. You probably already appreciate that you have to pay tradesmen for their time, whether they are working or not. You do not want anyone standing around. Imagine what it feels like to start worrying about paying people to stand around waiting when you would prefer to be ready to start looking for tenants.

Trades-people often have more than one job on at any one time so they are always juggling. Remember to any trade, time is money. We have to respect that. Time lost can prevent them from completing someone else's job and may mean they cannot pay their team. Emergencies can and do happen, so your preferred plumber may have to dash off at short notice and you may have no idea when your job is going to start again. If you repeatedly change your mind, after you have hired a particular trade, you are costing them valuable time and probably making them reluctant to work with you again.

Don't be the one whom they regard as least priority. You can make yourself the client they are willing to drop everything else for. I know you are wondering how. I know you are eager to have all the answers right now, but no-one can take it all in at once. Let's wait until we unleash our workforce.

Key points to remember
• Things can and do go wrong sometimes - accept it • Stick with the knitting. Do the things you are good at • Under-estimating initial funding can be painful • Draw down money only when you need it • Make the most of your own precious time • Respect trades-people's time. Don't waste it

CHAPTER 2 JUST IMAGINE

Just for a moment, imagine that you can avoid a great many (not all) of the things that can go wrong. By using a straight forward process you can do just that. Can you imagine what it would be like to have:

- A really good idea of the true cost of your project before you start?
- A really good idea of how long it will take and when it will complete?
- Confidence in the standard and quality of the finished project?
- Peace of mind and sleep at night (that's the big one)?
- The opportunity to learn from other people's mistakes?
- More time for yourself and those you care about?

GOOD IDEA OF COSTS

It can be really helpful to anticipate how much money you are going to spend in order to transform a property from the state it is in when you get hold of it, to the standard you want so that you can let it out to good tenants or to sell on. Imagine being able to say in advance *when* you expect to need funds for each aspect of the project. That way you only borrow money when you need it and not before. What might it feel like to be paying no more interest on money you might borrow too soon? Imagine being able to let your Joint Venture Partners know, at that very beginning, just how much the project will cost, when you will need their money, how much you are prepared to pay in interest and exactly when they will get their money back.

EFFICIENT USE OF TIME

Just imagine being in a position to predict with confidence when your project is going to finish. You can then start marketing (either to let it out or sell it on) even before the property is ready to be seen. What if you could be more relaxed, confidently knowing who should be where, when. Imagine never having to pay to have trades-people to stand around waiting to get on with whatever specific tasks they are hired to do?

Imagine feeling comfortable with whatever part of the project you are doing, confident that you have the right people and the right materials in the right place at the right time. Imagine the feeling of knowing you are making the best use of your own time and other people's time.

CONFIDENCE IN THE QUALITY

If you are confident in your trades-people and the standard of finish, imagine how easy it is going to be to market your property even before the works are completed. Consider how happy your joint venture partner or lender is going to be when they are kept in the picture and can see the standard to which the property is being refurbished. Such confidence can help reassure investors. They may be concerned about getting their money back on time, which depends on the quality of the property you aim to deliver to market. Good news travels fast. Future projects will become more attractive to prospective investors or lenders once you have a good track record of delivering good quality decent homes for decent people.

SLEEP WELL

Think what it is going to feel like when you have confidence in what needs to be done, when it is going to happen, what it is going to cost and that the finished standard is going to be to your taste. Think what it will be like to have fewer problems as you refurbish your property. Think of having everyone on the project happily working with you. You'll most likely sleep well, have more time for your family and friends and be able to secure funds for those things you want to do in the future.

LEARN FROM OTHER PEOPLE'S MISTAKES

Yes you can. You don't need to learn Project Management inside out; that is unless you intend to make a career of it. As a property investor, property owner or landlord, you just need to take advantage of the mistakes others have made, the situations that I and others have faced and the lessons I have learned, in my case, from around 20 years of managing mostly property projects.

You'll become aware later that becoming an investor/ landlord, managing property refurbishments wasn't originally part of my master plan for life. Perhaps that is a lesson in itself which you will be more than able to understand by the time you have read the rest of this guide. I travelled a bumpy road and took several side turns before I found what I really wanted to do to make a living. Slowly but surely I developed a way of managing what I was doing in a simplified and pragmatic manner.

Even devotees of one of the most widely used project management methodologies in public sector and construction projects in the UK, are starting to see that a flexible approach can be beneficial.

All I can share with you is my own simplified, practical process for managing property refurbishment projects. It calls on formal project management methodologies which I had to use in my day job, but involves a lot less form filling. It calls on what I have learned from other property people's mistakes. It also refers to my own mistakes. Some may amuse, but most I trust will help you avoid similar pitfalls.

It's not just each refurbishment project that you need to manage in order to save your valuable time, money and mental energy. The PUMA process can be used as a framework to manage your personal property journey; you'll see how later.

Successful business people save their own time and reap the benefits of the mistakes made by those who have gone before them. After all there is little point in reinventing the wheel.

Key points to remember
• Be prepared to learn from your own and others' mistakes • A pragmatic approach can be beneficial • Life and projects often take twists and turns – it's OK • Learn from other people's mistakes • Be confident about future costs, time and quality of your project – Yes you can, with a little help

Perhaps at this point I should give you an idea of how I eventually became a property project manager (a PM for short), so that you can see how anyone who wants to (that definitely includes you) can learn to manage their own property projects, regardless of background or career path.

CHAPTER 3 BECOMING A PROPERTY PM

Once you have made the decision to manage your own property refurbishments, it would be only natural for you to get advice from someone who has been there before you. It is my aim to help you here by introducing you to a simplified property project process. I've done the small two up, two down light refurbishments, managed projects in the private and public sectors and I've also been a project manager on some larger projects, so I reckon I may have something there to help you.

If I give you an idea of how I learned the skills and gained the right experience, you will most likely hope that you will not have to take so long. You won't. By learning from my experience and my mistakes you can arm yourself with a simple property project process. You too will know what to do to get that project done on time, within budget and to the quality standard you envisaged at the outset. This will give you the opportunity to sell or rent out your property at a price you determine and in a timely fashion.

Like many "project managers", my career started out along the IT route, peppered with exposure to mortgage finance, training / development and business administration, with a dash of my stubborn personality to garnish. If you have experience of any sort of projects, book keeping and accounts, mortgages, running a business or working with people, you will have a head start when it comes to managing property projects and achieving success in an enjoyable career alongside other investor landlords in the UK.

LEARNING ALONG THE WAY

My journey was far from straightforward. I made mistakes. I learned along the way. I met discouragement and encouragement in equal measure. It took some serious investment in training to get me off first base. Maybe you can relate to some of this. Maybe you, like me, didn't set out to become an investor landlord or property project manager; you may have fallen into to the role or had it dropped upon you. Whether you have a head start, are set on making property part of your future career, or find yourself following a path in property that requires you to know at least something about project management, my experiences will, I truly believe, help you grow, develop some solid relationships and have fun along the way.

SLEEPING ON THE JOB

My job, when working for a large building society supposedly calculating mortgage arrears (by hand), may seem an unlikely start. It did, however, get me summoned to the manager's office to be questioned one afternoon when I had fallen asleep, slumped across a ledger. At 17 years old, being summoned to speak with the manager felt like facing a firing squad.

Was I bored? I admitted it. Would you like to be one of the first to work with our new accounting machine – an IBM computer? Would I? Much better than getting fired. Sure! So I started as a computer operator in 1968 and became a programmer in 1971. As a lone female (as the local paper branded me) I spent over 10 years in IT (Information Technology). Eventually I left that building society to develop my line management skills in the City of London, working for an international reinsurance broker.

After a few years as a systems team leader and business analyst, I was promoted to become an IT project manager. Beware, there are far fewer "people" problems in IT than there are for a property project manager. In those days computer people were all believed to be bright young things. Egos ran high, but we all had the same attitude - lads together (even as a girl), hard-working, slightly mad, creative and self-motivated (which some trades-people and estate agents are not). With such a mix of like-minded young people it is comparatively easy to understand where another team member is coming from. Almost all our problems and passionate discussions could generally be resolved over a beer at the end of the working day.

In contrast property people are all so very varied. Age, gender, race, social background, intelligence, academic or physical skills, good or bad communicators, all feature in the complex and exciting world of property. This was one of the earliest lessons I learned when I first became an investor landlord.

Learning to deal with all the different people involved in a property project is a subject all to itself, although I will touch on it as we work through the property refurbishment process.

PICKING UP THE GAUNTLET

Picking up the gauntlet was perhaps, one of my greatest weaknesses. Sucker or adrenalin junkie is a label about which you might want to make up your own mind.

Accepting a new challenge first time around was actually great fun. If someone says they bet you can't do it as well as they can, the sucker in me goes "wanna bet?" Have you ever felt like that?

When my computer programming running mate at the building society wanted to do an Open University degree, the defiant streak in me came to the fore. We'd had a couple of programming head to head trials (just for fun) that always came out more or less equal. Sound bizarre? In the 1970s anyone "in computers" had to be some sort of whacky maverick. So getting an Open University degree would be just as much fun. It was. I saw an opportunity, set about achieving my degree in under 3 years, picked up the gauntlet and attained my first degree, on time, within budget and good enough.

In spite of put downs from friends and family who think "people like us" don't do degrees and that to even have such ideas is above our station, my running mate and I both completed the courses and got our degrees.

Not everyone around you will see things in the same way you do and certainly those closest to me did not see why a working class girl like me should think they had any right to get a degree, or indeed become a project manager or investor landlord. It hurts. You have to deal with it. Put downs got me on the road to a personal “can do” attitude. You can’t buy a “can do” attitude on eBay. You can develop one if you mix with like-minded people and read the right books.

Managing a property refurbishment project is little different from doing a degree project. There are several similarities, for example:

- You see the opportunity
- You set your own goals and budget
- Friends and family may laugh and tell you that sort of thing is “not for you” (unless you are truly fortunate in having positive understanding people all around you)
- You pick up the gauntlet, armed with what I’m going to show you in the following chapters
- Success comes within reach

MANAGEMENT TRAINING - BIG BIZ STYLE

Initiation into the world of project management: what did that look like? A one day course on the use of MsProject and I was let loose running a few projects. Powerful and useful as MsProject is, I find it difficult to imagine anyone learning to use it to best advantage in one day. Trial and error can take up a great deal of your time. If you want to learn how to get the best out of any such powerful software, get yourself on a good course. If I had my time over again I would find a course that includes a great deal of practical work with a tutor on hand. I'd swear by the use of project management software tools to help keep track of any project lasting longer than, say, 3 months. The majority of public sector and construction projects do.

Me? I bungled along for around 10 years, managing systems projects and learning both the quirks of MsProject and the practicalities of project management, by osmosis.

MOST REWARDING PROJECT

My most rewarding project was a two year project with my team of 20 -30 people at any one time, bringing together several accounting systems onto one company-wide system. The predicted financial benefits (a critical success factor – but more of that later) became reality sooner than anticipated, after which I was bored again and open to new challenges.

GROTTY BASEMENT TO TRAINING FACILITY

The next project was to refurbish part of the basement of an office block and turn it into what was then a high tech IT training facility. Challenges such as smelly drains, windows that opened onto a brick wall, integrated projection, diverse computer types and finding somewhere to fit in a preparation room and storage for all that hard copy training course material, gave me a good grounding in managing refurbishments. With little experience of carpenters, electricians, equipment suppliers, wiring diagrams, locksmiths, plumbers, building control or interpersonal conflicts, you can imagine the mistakes and rework that had to be done. Rework is always costly in both time and money.

Lesson learned? Practical training in whatever you are about to do is worthwhile and can save you years of mistakes. Learning from other people's mistakes is priceless, which is where this guide comes in. Life is too short for you to wait 10 years.

CAUGHT NAPPING AGAIN

Taking a nap one afternoon (I was bored again and using up my annual leave), a job agency phoned me to see if I was interested in a large building project at a local school, managing the IT/ electrical infrastructure installation, on a lucrative contract. What do you think I said? Of course I was. I seized (whilst trying to sound cool) the opportunity and consequently topped up my property project knowledge in a big way. The school wanted my experience and what I could deliver for them in return for nothing more than money. A fair exchange, wasn't it? While I was there I made a point of learning from other people about bigger building projects, architect's drawings, and site security, working with larger contractors and diverse multiple stakeholders.

Lesson learned? In bigger organisations the outcomes for the organisation take priority over the needs of hired hands such as I was at that time. Results and fire-fighting the everyday challenges, are often top priority for any large organisation. Saving money is equally important. On this assignment competition among permanent employees meant knowledge was not freely shared; knowledge is power and everyone wants to get on, sometimes at the expense of others.

PROPERTY PEOPLE SHARE KNOW HOW

Unlike working for a large organisation, in the property business there is a wealth knowledge and a wide diversity of experience *freely shared*. Property people, including myself, enjoy seeing other property people succeed and are happy to share what they have learned. You are never alone. As I share my experience with you, I look forward to hearing about your success one day.

I reckon the pains of learning how to manage projects in big business has enabled me to take what is of good practical use and adapt it to the investor landlord's business; this I can gladly pass on to you.

FIT OF PIQUE

When I bought my first buy to let, a simple two up, two down, terrace house that was rather an eyesore in a run-down district, I had zero property investment experience, but I had successfully refurbished that dingy old basement, remember, so why not? At that time no-one had explained to me how to make money by buying the most run down property in the *best* location one could afford. Even if you cannot change its location you can improve the standard of a property.

It was in a fit of pique regarding the level at which my meagre savings interest was being taxed that I made this initial purchase. Having been made redundant 3 times (this was when IT became mainstream and "professional") in the wake of the rise in outsourcing and decline of the global economy (which a cyclical thing just like the property market), I was able to buy the cheapest freehold property I could find on the market in Kent, for cash. I later learned there are better ways to buy property when you are starting out; please note!

What did I do wrong with this first investment property?

- No due diligence
- No idea if the price was reasonable
- No attempt at negotiation
- No idea if anyone would want to live in that location
- No idea what the rent should be
- No idea what sort of people rent in that area
- No idea what my exit strategy was
- All my eggs in one basket (I'd spent all my money on one property)

A higher power must have been watching over me when I started out because after my first botched up refurbishment and enduring some horrendous tenants I doubled my money when it came to sell up. I started investing in a better way. Had I initially used my money to leverage additional funds I could have acquired three or more properties and even more money in the bank more rapidly to fund my retirement.

BEWARE OF SOMEONE ELSE'S AGENDA

When I was running a small IT training unit, one of the tutors had ambitions to run his own management training company. He needed a business degree to be seen as credible. During his appraisal I asked him how I could help him achieve his long term goal while satisfying the shorter term goals of the company and our training unit. He suggested we study for an MBA at the same time, side by side. It was a much longer series of conversations than that, but I won't bore you with the manipulative details here. It sounded like fun and that sucker in me picked up the gauntlet (again). Company politics and corporate human insecurities were not understood by the naive me at all. I just wanted to have fun.

What he omitted to say was that we should both study the same MBA course (self-study 15 hours from spare time each week and one weekend with the tutors each month) and *I should fail*. Then he could be seen as better than me, then have my job as a stepping stone to his longer term goal! The sucker in me picked up the gauntlet and worked hard for two years to get my second degree.

The other fellow? I can never be certain but as far as I know he gave up!

BUSINESS AWARENESS

What did that two years do for me? Quite a lot really. Well I got my degree, but that was little use in the company I worked for at the time. Gender equality was yet to emerge.

Corporate strategy, organisational politics, financial accounting all started to interest me and make sense and even excite me. In the early days of my property journey I read everything I could about financial planning, financial and management accounting and tax, just so that I could do my own book keeping until I had sufficient cash flow to hire someone else.

With growing confidence I realised that I could run my own business (maybe a property business) and that I may need to leave behind the past, including some people that held me back. This is one of the key lessons, especially in the property business, where it is not uncommon for friends and family to (unwittingly) hold you back.

Visualise your life in the future. See the end game and focus on how you are going to get there. Determine what needs to be done. That's the start point of any corporate strategy.

Preparation of a "G Incorporated" business plan, followed by several years of property investing and refurbishment started to cause a subtle change among the many doubters. Other people's jealousy, however unintentional, can hold you back in much the same way that it creeps into larger organisations; we call it politics.

PROPERTY BUSINESS TRAINING

No, I did not have the courage to leave *too* much of my past behind. Had I known then what I know now I would have handed in my notice and said good bye to my JOB right there and then. But I was scared. If you are scared of letting go, that's normal. All I can say is that once I eventually did let go (feel the fear and do it anyway) it was the start of a property career that has given me all I ever wanted. Nowadays I do have time to sit and gaze at my garden and say "this is what I worked for and I am happy".

I continued working as an employee for a while, managing projects for other people. Now there is an opportunity for you too, but not as an employee. Managing property projects for other people, as part of your own business, can earn you a decent living, coupled with the freedom to control your own destiny. But, you will need additional training, not neglecting the people skills, to market your services and deliver in a way that exceeds your customer expectations.

INSPIRATION FROM SOME OF THE BEST

Yes, I did do something sensible to move forward the idea of a property business; I took a week long intensive property investment course where I met the wonderful lady who would inspire me to put my property knowledge, business knowledge and project management experience together for myself. Gill became a mentor and remains a role model for me.

In so many ways I wish I had taken that property training earlier. Learning from seasoned property investors, experienced landlords and professional builders was most certainly exhausting, immense fun and a great foundation. Just one day out looking at around half a dozen properties with a builder, being helped to see what needed to be done to bring each property up to scratch and estimating how much it might cost to do the refurbishment, was worth the entire course fee in itself. At that time buy to let, buying from motivated sellers, or refurbishing distressed property was almost the only way to go. Understanding the real secret of why it is more lucrative to use other people's cash as leverage than to buy your first property outright, kicked me up the proverbial.

ACTION TIME

It was action time, even for a rather cautious person! Fortunately property prices were on the rise as that recession passed (economies thrive in cycles) so when I sold that little terraced place in the wrong location, it easily provided deposits for my next few property investments in the Medway towns. That is what I mean by leverage. You can use your own savings, or a partner's money to find the minimum deposit, then borrow the rest on an interest only basis. Borrowing can be a mortgage, a joint venture partner's loan, a loan from crowd funding or any other type of loan.

In this guide, we are going to focus on a simple process for managing the refurbishment of a property, not the leveraged way to go about investing (that is for another day perhaps)

MAKE USE OF WHAT YOU LEARN

So, the Davis Hornsby property business simply ticked along fairly smoothly and steadily. It is surprising how beneficial it was to my property business to make use of what I learned through seemingly unrelated training. What I had learned about finance, cash flow forecasting, business planning, organisational politics, marketing, business law, business insurance, human resource management, reporting, budgeting and innovation, all helped get my property dabbling onto a professional business footing.

Whatever your past, you have learned so much; the unique skills you have already mastered will almost certainly help you in your property journey.

Never under estimate the value of training. Continuing professional development can be, but need not exclusively be, by attendance at short courses and seminars. Networking meetings, reading relevant magazines and taking out membership of a professional property association are really inexpensive ways of topping up your property education in what is an ever changing property climate.

LEAP OF FAITH

After a few positive but difficult life changes I hankered after the freedom of not being an employee. At the same time, the apparent security of an employer (don't be fooled as I was) still tried to seduce me. Your notice period, typically one to three months, is the only security there is with an employer.

Freedom versus security! Does that sound familiar to you?

Maybe you have been there. Maybe you don't feel appreciated in the job you are doing. Maybe you are not a political animal and you are not getting the promotion you deserve. Perhaps you are feeling that way now. Such conflicts are often the trigger to turn your life around.

So when I got that phone call asking me if I was interested in a one year contract as an IT and electrical infrastructure project manager for a new build study centre at a well-respected school, I took a leap of faith, resigned from employment and immersed myself in managing one of the most exciting projects I have done. Some gauntlets are worth picking up, especially if they are a good fit for the life you deserve. That project taught me a great deal about building contracts, planning, plant hiring, insurance, welfare facilities, CDM (Construction Design and Management), architects, the role of the clerk of works, the practical differences between drawings that pass planning / building regulations and the challenges you'll have to face on the ground, plus a whole lot more, some of which I have already mentioned. Believe me, there was no shortage of challenges and things going wrong.

Lesson learned! *Something will go wrong on any project. What is important is how you deal with it.*

THE JOB LEFT BEHIND

Once that project assignment was completed I had to choose between making a living from residential property and getting another "proper" job (that's it – you've heard it before – JOB = just over broke). Having taken the leap of faith, walked away from a JOB, bought, done up and sold several residential units, I guess I was by then qualified to call myself an investor/ landlord and property refurbishment project manager.

You now know how I started out. So, how can *you* get started? After recapping on the key points to remember from this chapter, you'll soon see. Think about where *you* want to go.

Key points to remember
• Don't worry if friends or family tell you this is not for you • Property people love to share knowledge and information, unlike in almost any other industry • Sometimes you have to leave the past behind • Never spend all your cash on your first property • Whatever your past, the skills you already have will serve you well • Never under-estimate the value of training • When things go wrong, what is important is how you deal with it

CHAPTER 4 START WITH THE END IN MIND

LEARN FROM THE PUMA

Would you not agree, the puma is a magnificent animal? I love those wildlife / big cat type TV shows. Maybe that's what made me think how a property refurbishment project is so like a big cat's hunt for dinner. My inspiration in developing this simplified project process came, in part, from my admiration for the puma.

When a puma is looking for her next dinner, perhaps a tasty gazelle, she knows exactly what she intends the *outcome* of her efforts to be. She knows a few key things before the hunt begins.

- She knows exactly *what* she must do
- She looks at the specific hunt, works out *what she is going to do and how*
- She knows her own *stamina*
- She is prepared to *adapt* tactics to circumstances
- She knows when to stop the hunt and call it a day, if circumstances dictate (e.g. in our case, legislation)

You and I need to know such things too.

When we are looking at starting a property refurbishment, perhaps a small house or a couple of flats, we need to know what the *outcome* of our efforts will be. We need to visualise the end result. We need to know exactly *what* we must do to get there. Most of our effort will go into the first stage of our refurbishment project. This is to work out *what we are going to do and how*. We need to set a *budget* too. We must also have an exit strategy so that we know whether or not to call it a day if we cannot achieve all we want within the budget we have set. Can you see the similarities?

The puma has learned from those who have "done it" before, that is her sisters, aunts and Mother. She knows how to read the landscape, how to close the kill and the alternative options. She has learned what is achievable and what is not since she was a young cub. She knows how to go about the chase, the kill and how to deal with the reward from years of learning from her own experience and the experience of others.

Every young puma also learns what works best for her and is always ready to adapt.

Learn from others and be ready to adapt to circumstances.

Project planning has a lot in common with the puma's preparation for the hunt.

Once the chase is on, she monitors every changing move of her prey and slightly adjusts her tactics until she gets the kill. Having rested a while she looks back at how the hunt went, learns from what happened and uses that knowledge when hunting for the next meal.

Learning from the puma gave me the idea of using PUMA as an acronym, standing for **P**lan, **U**nleash, **M**onitor and **A**nalyse.

Visualise, plan and unleash the hunting forces. Monitor how it went, analyse what happened and plan the next hunt / project stage.

The puma hunting her prey will start with the end in mind. Stephen Covey strongly advises successful people to "start with the end in mind". So, start out by visualising exactly what the refurbished property will look like, who is going to live there, what standard it is going to be in order to attract the right customer (buyer or tenant). You need to d*ecide who your ideal customer is first.*

Just in case you cannot relate to the puma, can you visualise going away on a well-earned holiday? I doubt you'd set off without knowing where you are going, who you want to go with, how you are going to get there, what insurance you may need, what currency to take, what it will cost, what vaccinations to have or what clothes to pack. Try one day! I doubt you will have the holiday you hoped for. The same is true of a property refurbishment project.

So what am I talking about? The need to plan.

Your key objective is to get your refurbishment done,

ON TIME, ON BUDGET AND TO YOUR PREDEFINED STANDARDS.

LEARN FROM DR STEPHEN COVEY

Habit two of Stephen Covey's book "The 7 Habits of Highly Effective People" asserts that to succeed you must know what the end is going to look like, as I said. What are your properties going to be like? What sort of people are going to live in your properties? He uses the example of asking a child what he wants to be when he grows up. Managing a property refurbishment is very much the same. What do you want your property to be when its refurbishment is complete?

Stephen Covey even suggests that what he calls a personal mission statement is just about the best way to achieve what you want to do. You may recall my mention of writing "G. Incorporated" as a business plan. The very first section outlines my mission statement. It includes what I want to do with my life and my property journey. It's my personal plan. You could do worse than develop your own personal mission statement. Just for a moment think about what it would say.

You could do worse than jot down your first thoughts on your property journey and what it will enable you to achieve and how it might secure your future. In fact it is a recipe for failure if you set out on your property journey with no idea of where you are going; that is *unless* you are prepared to learn and adapt.

- Are you willing to see what you are doing wrong?
- Are you able to analyse what you can do about it?

- Will you write down what you are trying to achieve?
- Will you write down what the end is going to look like?
- Are you willing to work out how you are going to get to your destination?
- Do you know how to measure whether or not you have ended up with what you want?

BE MASTER OF YOUR OWN DESTINY

Beware what someone else wants for you, however noble it may be at the time. Beware of someone else's vision (ambition) for your success. When I was a child, my own father had ambitions for me, to be a successful personal assistant (PA) to someone in the corporate world. The more books I read and the more successful property entrepreneurs I mixed with, the more my vision of the end game developed. Today I am my own boss. As my own boss I can hire a virtual PA when I need one. When you are your own boss, the success of your projects is the key to your survival, just as the puma must succeed in the kill in order to eat and survive.

STAY FOCUSSED

When you make that decision to undertake property projects, which almost inevitably will incorporate some element of refurbishment, staying focussed and having a clear picture of what the specific outcomes are going to be, are both vital to your success. In the corporate world, such outcomes tend to be referred to as critical success factors.

By asking at the outset, right at the beginning of the project, what the property is going to look like and what standard it is going to be, the probability of your success is very much increased.

For example, for those of you who like a bit of spontaneity, I'd remind you that if you have a clear picture, right at the beginning and remain focussed, you are able to avoid inconvenience and overrunning on both time and cost.

So the first thing in my project process is to have a clear vision of exactly what a project will look like when completed, what steps are involved and how to actually do the project.

By approaching your project systematically, the probability of your success is truly very much increased. That is why we do the first stage in the four stages in this project process. What am I taking about? You know the answer to that one, don't you? I'm talking about planning. If you are not serious and are reluctant to do sufficient planning, please don't expect to truly succeed.

If you plan and *manage* your project planning properly, you cannot truly be said to fail. Adapting to changing circumstances in the way the puma does during the hunt is not failing; it is well thought out decision making and good management. Call it good hunting if you prefer.

Key points to remember
• Picture your ideal customer first • Have a completely clear picture of the finished property before you start • Focus on your goals • Visualise your outcomes, plan, monitor how it is going, analyse the situation and plan your next steps • Know what you have to do before you start • Your objective is to complete your project on time, within your budget and to your own pre-determined standard • **P**lan, **U**nleash, **M**onitor and **A**nalyse

CHAPTER 5 PLAN – SCOPE & DOCUMENTATION

SCOPE

Before you even start to plan, you need to have a picture of what the end result of your project. You need to know exactly what it is you are going to end up with, in the same way the puma knows what her dinner should look like: nice juicy young gazelle large enough to feed her and her cubs. Picture it.

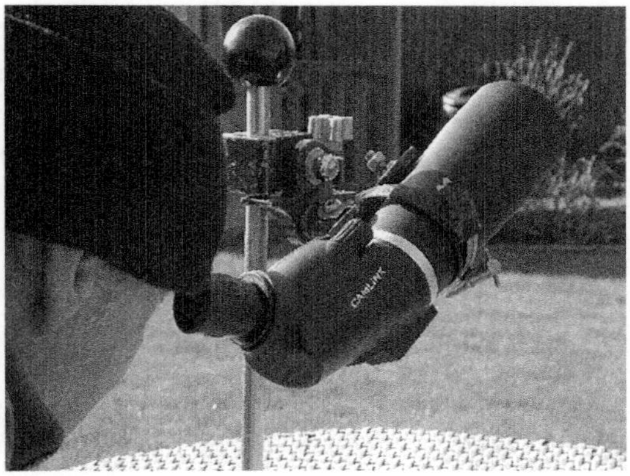

It is as if you are looking through a telescope to the future for something you hope to see, ignoring anything in your peripheral vision.

Similarly, this is why we start with what we call a scoping document. What is that? It is simply something written down that defines the scope of the project. It defines exactly what your project will deliver, the "deliverables".

Why write it down? To give you a framework and prevent the project overrunning on time or budget, just because you changed your mind part way through. Write it down and stay within the scope you set. When you stray outside the defined scope of any project, we call that "project creep"; it is costly and can cause delays.

Now it need not be a time consuming or a very formal thing; it all depends on who the stakeholders are, that is those people with a vested interest in the project. If the project is funded by joint venture investors you may have to be more formal and provide more detail than if the only stakeholder is you and perhaps a partner.

- Are you going to do a quick clean and paint job simply to make the property look smart so that you can get it on the market quickly?
- Are you going to fully modernise the entire property and finish it to a very high standard in order to achieve the best price?
- Are you intending to make a one bedroom apartment into a two bedroom apartment and maximise your profit?
- What sort of customer are you doing this for?
- Are you providing basic homes for decent people?
- Are you creating student accommodation?
- Are you providing serviced accommodation for executives or travelling professionals?
- Are you creating a superior home for sale?
- Are you providing a safe home for an elderly person or couple?
- Could your property become a holiday let?

The possibilities are almost endless.

BALL PARK BUDGET AND TIME FRAME

Once you know what it is going to look like, you'll need to decide on a ball park budget and time frame, that is to say your best estimate. Both of these will be refined at a later stage of the project process.

CRITICAL SUCCESS FACTORS

Since you need to be able to step back and check what you actually get done against your vision, you need to write down those things which are critical to you. They are the project's critical success factors (CSFs). So many people omit to include them, or mistake them for targets. A target is something you aim for. A critical success factor is something you *must* achieve in order to regard the project as a success. How can you say your project was a success if you failed to set down at the outset those factors which *must* be delivered? There would be nothing to compare to, would there?

WHEN TO DEFINE THE SCOPE

Think about who are you going to be accountable to for achieving whatever it is you set out to do? Yourself? Someone who has hired you to manage his / her project? Your bank? A joint venture partner? You are accountable to someone and you have to define what is included and what is not.

Typically the project scoping document is written first, then later enhanced as other aspects of your project come together. If you intend to hire a project manager to run your property project, then the scoping document is what you as owner and primary stakeholder of the project will need to provide. By providing a clear scope for the project, a good project manager will be able to work out a reliable price and timescale for his / her services.

A scoping document defines:

- why the project is being undertaken
- what the outcomes of the project will be
- the key elements which must be included in the project
- how much the project should cost at most
- how the project is to be funded
- when the project will start and when it will finish
- who the stakeholders are
- what is excluded from the project – this is crucial
- if the project is to be undertaken in phases, what each phase will achieve
- how the success or otherwise of the project will be measured (critical success factors or CSFs)

As an example, imagine planning to "do up" a one bed flat to rent out. Once you are happy the rental numbers stack up, after doing your due diligence, the scope may simply be no more than a short note or memo. It might say something such as:

"The project will provide a home for professionals, with a good standard of understated décor and an expected rent of £x (see rightmove.co.uk) per calendar month.

The property will be rewired and re-plumbed. A new kitchen and bathroom will be installed to drawings provided, all rooms being re-plastered and painted in neutral shades and warm white gloss wood work. Contract standard carpets will be professionally fitted to all rooms, except the kitchen and bathroom which will have new vinyl flooring fitted.

Health and safety must be taken into account in all final fittings. All necessary compliance certificates will be obtained.

Double glazing and central heating to be serviced not replaced.

A budget of £xx,xxx is anticipated, with a limit of £xx,xxx, provided as a loan from Joe Bloggs. Complete the project, ready to market within12 weeks. Start date is set for 01/mm/yyyy. Progress, including costs so far, will be reported to Joe Bloggs at a weekly face to face meeting.

Critical success factors include:

- Completion ready to market within the timeframe
- Actual costs within the budget limit
- Property is health and safety compliant
- Independent assessment of rent potential congruent with that expected, so that Joe Bloggs can be repaid from the rent within six months"

This is just an example for a very small project. Joe Bloggs is the only stakeholder other than the owner, whom I have assumed to be the acting project manager in this simplified example. This is typical of projects undertaken by many residential property investor / landlords, before they take on greater things.

The scope will of course differ in its detail depending on the size and state of the property. Whether you are about to refurbish a one bedroomed flat or undertake conversion of a large property into flats or an HMO (home in multiple occupancy), the principles are the same. The project process is the same.

FORMAL SCOPING

When I have prepared scoping documents for larger projects in the corporate world, they have included an outline work plan (more of that shortly), included many stakeholders, identified a project board and ended up some tens of pages long. For most typical residential property refurbishment projects, I'd tend to keep to no more than two pages. It does depend on the size of the project and who you are answerable to.

If you are hiring a project manager or a main building contractor, the scoping document tends to be called a design specification and ought to contain far greater detail; it tells the person responsible for the project what you want doing, over what timeframe and at what sort of budget. A mood board with colours and fabric or paint samples is often attached for clarity. The document helps someone clearly see what you need doing and what is within the scope of the project and what is not.

There is a lot to think about when defining the scope of a project, but not necessarily a great deal to write down. It is the thinking it through process that helps you move forward with confidence. Think first and be clear on the scope of the project.

WHAT DO YOU NEED TO DOCUMENT?

Unless you are superman / woman or your refurbishment project is extremely limited, you'll need to get something written down. That's documentation. I'll assume you are going to do more than just a clean of the property, so we need to look at what you have to document in one way or another. We have already looked at how brief the scope might be, but it still needs to be documented. Please, no groans.

That's right, I did say document, but it need not be onerous; after all, you do it every time you plan a holiday, don't you?

GET ORGANISED

When I plan a holiday I guess I am no different from you. I end up with a file of papers. Receipts, insurance documents, tickets, itinerary, maps and much more end up stuffed into a file. Do you then find it hard to lay your hands on that insurance emergency number when the tour operator asks for it? Maybe slightly better organised filing would help?

Running a property refurbishment project is very much the same, so we need documentation and it needs to be filed in an orderly and easily accessible fashion.

Different people file documents in different places. It often depends on who is going to need to find it. Without going into great detail, just a few alternatives include:

- Your own PC / Mac, for example as word processing or spreadsheet documents
- Paper file, locked away in a cabinet
- Dropbox or other cloud storage which allows you to share, perhaps with a business partner and stakeholders
- A memory stick or other external electronic media you can lock away in a safe

It's not only the actual tasks that have to be done that need to be documented. It is a start, but only the start of a work plan. If you are using a formal commercial project management process (remember that from my "job" days) as part of managing the project there are likely to be many, perhaps too many, documents; but I've learned to slim this down and simplify my approach. This simplified approach is what I am glad to be sharing with you; it will help you just as it helps me to keep control of my projects. Within my project approach there are no more than four *essential* documents to plan a refurbishment project and two of these can be very brief.

The essential four things I like to document are as follows:

- The Scope
- The Work Plan
- The Budget
- The Communications Plan

Once you have documented the scope, you now have a clear idea of *why* you are doing this refurbishment project, *what is and what is not* within the scope of the works and what the finished property is going to look like.

Are you starting to feel more comfortable? You should.

Knowing *what* is one thing. Knowing *how* to get there is another. It's time to start planning the actual work, the actual tasks. Why? Well, imagine if you don't plan the work what chaos might ensue.

Fail to plan and you plan to fail.

If you've read this far, you have already increased the probability of your projects completing successfully. Reward yourself, before we move on to a more detailed process for planning each project.

Perhaps you have already been through an unplanned project and become familiar with some chaos! Before we get more serious and take a detailed look at planning the actual tasks, let's take a breath and recap.

Key points to remember
• Document the project scope so that you can compare the outcomes as you progress and at the project end • Define what you intend to deliver • Specify what is included in, and what is specifically excluded from the project • Include those factors that are critical to successful completion of your project - CSFs • Keep documentation where everyone involved can readily find it – be an organised puma • Fail to plan and you plan to fail

CHAPTER 6 PLAN – THE WORK PLAN

THE WORK PLAN

Once you have a clear idea of the scope of your project and have that written down, let's look at the work plan. Why? Well, by starting with the work plan and looking at just five key components of any plan, you will be in a good position to work up a sound budget, remind yourself and show other people how you are going to run this project.

How can you budget, know when to stop, or let other people know what is going on if you haven't thought out the plan for the actual tasks within your project? It would be like going away on holiday without the right clothes, money or the tickets and not knowing which airport or railway station to go to or when you might arrive. Perhaps you thrive on uncertainty but stakeholders and trades-people are unlikely to. They must be able to reference a work plan. You too, need a work plan.

So, *what* exactly are you going to put into your initial work plan? The more thoroughly you plan the more likely the project is to run smoothly. Put the effort in at this stage and everything else follows on logically. I use an acronym to help me.

Just remember to TREAD carefully.

It will help you remember the five key steps in preparing a work plan for your project.

- **T**asks
- **R**esources
- **E**stimates
- **A**llow for Contingencies
- **D**ependencies

LIST TASKS IN YOUR WORK PLAN

Make a list of every task that will need to be done to complete the project. Any order will do at this point in time. Some tasks should be broken down into several smaller tasks. e.g. "Rip Out The Old" should be broken down into tasks such as "remove old electrics", "disconnect gas", "demolish old fitted wardrobes", "take out old bathroom", "dispose of rubbish from site". Why? Because they use different skills and different people, but most can be done at the same time.

Aim to make no defined task take more than five days. This makes it easier to see exactly where you are in the project and how things are going. It also makes it easier to dovetail people into time slots for each task. For now just take my word for it and aim to make each specific task last no more than five days.

JOT DOWN THREE THINGS FOR EACH TASK

In our practical workshop you can practise what I am about to describe. Let's look at the first three things against each task in developing a work plan.

- Write down *a meaningful name* for each task you can think of which is going to be done
- Against each one write down *how long you think* it will take in number of days effort
- Try to break any task you think will take more than five days into *shorter tasks*

Sounds simple, doesn't it? Simple is not always easy.

Don't forget the initial tasks to get the project underway – the project set-up. These might include getting approval for the plan from other people involved, getting local authority planning consents, confirming where your funds are coming from, getting building regulations consent, dealing with party wall legislation and even getting the keys if you are acquiring the property or seeing previous tenants out.

COMFORT, HEALTH AND SAFETY RESPONSIBILITY

Let's not forget health and safety tasks. UK law places a duty of care on you to ensure the property is fit for people to live in at the beginning of a tenancy if you intend to rent the property out. Electrical safety and gas safety are both crucial. Insulation and the energy performance of the property are equally important, not only for the comfort and affordability of your tenants (or buyers) but also because you *must* make a current EPC (Energy Performance Certificate) available when you put the property on the market.

You'll also need to include specific tasks necessary to provide a safe environment for anyone working on the property / properties. We'll look at that in more detail later, when we consider the welfare of your work force.

BODY OF THE WORK PLAN

Then there is the "body" of the project. This might be broken down into phases if you feel that is appropriate. For example, if you have several flats in one building you can plan to do one at a time, then repeat. You need only break down one flat / phase into its individual tasks then copy and paste the tasks into the overall plan.

The group of tasks in this part of the work plan is rather like the actual lunch chase for the puma. It will include, among other things, taking out all the old fixtures and fittings you no longer require and disposing of them, ordering new materials, enlisting the services of trades-people to put it all back together again, decorating, fitting out and the dressing / presentation of the property for sale or rent.

MATERIALS AND SUPPLIERS

Include tasks for ordering materials, awaiting delivery and taking delivery. When considering ordering materials, you'll probably need different suppliers. Do bear in mind that lead times will differ across suppliers. Include tasks that allow for this. So, include one task for "order xyz", one for "await" and one for "take delivery of xyz". Your list of materials is likely to include things such as:

- kitchen units
- timber, screws, sealants, adhesives, nuts and nails
- plumbing supplies
- electrical supplies
- double glazing units
- white goods
- fillers, paint, brushes and other decorating materials
- floor coverings and soft furnishings

Landlords can not only get good deals from suppliers by direct negotiation, but can benefit via the Landlords National Property Group (LNPG.co.uk) and any other discount buying group.

PLAN A NEAT END TO YOUR PROJECT

Finally there are those tasks which neatly complete the project - the project closure. These might include final clean, building regulations sign off, compliance certification, repaying investors, re-financing, comparing outcomes against those critical success factors and evaluating how well, or not, the outcomes stacked up. Don't forget to include a task for a *post refurbishment review.*

The project completion meeting might be a meal, drinks or a formal signing off meeting, depending on your style and the nature of the project. The meeting will consider how you can improve the success of your projects in the future. This is the fun part where relationships are maintained for the longer term.

GET STRUCTURE INTO YOUR PLAN (SOFTWARE)

So far we have only talked about a simple list of just four high level project tasks.

- Project set up
- Health and Safety
- The meat / body of the refurbishment
- Project closure

In an ideal world you would ask yourself how long each of these is expected to take. From this basic outline it is rather a challenge to answer that question. Maybe now it is becoming a little clearer as to why we break each of these high level tasks down into smaller tasks. When each task is small enough to ask yourself or someone else "how long do we think this will take?" and expect a fairly accurate estimate, you are almost ready to look at *who* is going to work on each task.

I did say almost. If you have one long jumbled heap of tasks with absolutely no structure, then moving forward is going to be less than easy. So how can you start to get some structure into your work plan? I'll give you a couple of ways.

SPREADSHEET OR PROJECT MANAGEMENT SOFTWARE

Use of software can reduce future headaches no end. For very small projects I'd use Excel or some other spreadsheet software. For longer projects I prefer purpose designed project management software which has many more useful features. These include easy ways to:

- calculate time to complete
- calculate budget spent
- record work completed and time taken
- see where resources are over / under committed
- re-calculate the whole project to produce a new plan

When using any software start with our four tasks, key them in then for the next level of task breakdown, indent. Then for any further level of task breakdown, key the task on a new line and indent again. When the tasks need not be broken down further, key in the time each low level task is expected to take. We can do this in man days. Then let software add up the small task times to see how long each main task is estimated to take.

Although not designed as project management software, Excel has enough functionality to enable you to plan many a refurbishment project. I find it can be OK to use in order to develop my refurbishment project plans. Building in the simple formulas for adding up the planned and actual costs and durations is something you will have to do, but only once, then you can use your work plan as a model for your next project.

FIRST CUT WORK PLAN

I'll just show you an example in a moment. This is just a high level, first cut that you might start with. You will notice I have given each task a number and that the tasks are not necessarily in the most appropriate sequence - *yet*. Nor are the cost estimates particularly realistic; it depends what value you put on your own time.

You have to start with something.

A word of warning. Please don't try to do this in Word or use the old "fag packet" approach. Having been obliged to use Word to illustrate this for you in this guide, I promise you it is far easier and less time consuming to use a spreadsheet or project management software.

If you are unfamiliar with preparing a work plan, it will help you to critically study my deliberately flawed example in a minute. Go get a cup of coffee. Now see what you can glean. Make notes of any questions you may have and see how they begin to get answered as we work through the various stages of managing a refurbishment project.

	Task	Estimated Duration	Estimated Cost
		24.5 d	**£3,055**
1	Project set up	**7.5 days**	**£625**
1.1	Complete work plan	2 days	£100
1.2	Set up insurances	0.5 days	£25
1.3	Document Scope	1 day	£50
1.4	Stakeholders' meeting	1 day	£300
1.5	Prepare budget	2 days	£100
1.6	Assign H&S responsibility	1 day	£50
	Project all set up		
2	Refurb house		
2.1	Rip out the old	**5 days**	**£380**
2.1.1	Rip out kitchen	3 days	£180
2.1.2	Rip out bathroom	3 days	£200
	All old ripped out		
2.2	Actual refurb / renovation	**9 days**	**£1,800**
2.2.1	Replace plumbing	2 days	£400
2.2.2	Replace kitchen	4 days	£800
2.2.3	Replace bathroom	3 days	£600
	All new installed		
2.3	Project closure	**3 days**	**£250**
2.3.1	Post completion review	3 days	£250
	Ready for next project		

You can see from my over simplified and flawed outline work plan just how the costs start to mount up.

Notice that "Project closure" should not be a sub task of "Refurb house", so it should be numbered 3.

Notice that one two-day tasks does not necessarily cost the same as another two-day task. The plumber is likely to cost twice as much as whoever is preparing the budget. Remember to put a price on your own valuable time. Adding up costs and estimates can be automated using software.

Personally? Well, I do prefer the neatness and flexibility of a software prepared plan; I already have a reasonable idea of what tasks need to be done in a refurbishment and I am thinking of how previous projects have worked out. Using software means I can store my plan in cloud storage and simply email the link to people on my team.

Now, don't think this is a complete work plan. There are a few more steps before it becomes a proper work plan. Once some of the other parts of your work plan have been added, it will take better shape.

Remember, TREAD carefully. There are five steps remember.

- **T**asks
- **R**esources
- **E**stimates

- **A**llowance for contingencies
- **D**ependencies

After listing your tasks in *some sort* of structure, let's consider costs and who/ what skills or equipment you'll need.

RESOURCES FOR YOUR WORK PLAN

Consider money, relevant trades-people and professionals and determine where you can get the necessary equipment and materials from. Don't forget price. These are the resource types you'll need. *Think* about these together for each task in your work plan:

- Cost of each task
- The people with the right skill set
- Materials or equipment

We'll be looking at budgeting shortly, so let's go with a guestimate for the moment, based on your previous experience. Often, when project planning, we think of resources in terms of skills. If you already have your power team in place, great. If Fred X is your preferred carpenter, then use his initials, FX, in the plan. If not, just state carpenter, then find a good one and update the plan with their initials later.

So what do we do, either using software or some paper method of developing our plan?

Simply look at each low level task (those you anticipate taking five or less days). These are the right-most (most indented) and might be thought of as the leaves of a tree (on its side). Then ask three questions.

- Who (or what skill) do I need to get this task done?
- What materials will I need to get this task done?
- What do I think (given my past experience) this is going to cost?

In any actual project management software there will be a column for resources and a column for estimated cost. It is here you insert the initials (or skill if you do not yet have someone in mind) of the individual or company you plan to use, against each low level task. On a large project it is easy to over allocate an individual and have him (or the company), in theory, in several places at once. This is not a good idea! Project management software is invaluable in this respect as most packages have the facility to allocate a full time resource, half time or a percentage of their time and produce a report that shows you if you have made this sort of mistake. It can be set up to take into account weekends, public holidays and individual vacations. The software can, generally, reschedule the time frame to fit around the resources or tell you how many resources (e.g. electricians) you will need if you stick to the original dates.

If you are using a spreadsheet, have a column for resources. Against each low level task simply key in the resource initials, e.g. JB for Joe Bloggs. Where you need several, for example plumbers, say so by referring to them as plumber one, plumber two and so on.

You can build your spreadsheet up yourself or adapt the stacked bar chart template. Something like Excel is not really designed to be a project management tool so it lacks the functionality of purpose-built project management software. On the other hand, people have been using spreadsheets for project management and have built templates with some functionality. A Google search will throw up several templates with handy Youtube video clips to show you how to use them.

Some tasks need no materials. For example, if the task is "service existing gas boiler" you have allocated a Gas Safe boiler engineer so there is no need to provide any materials.

At the other extreme, if the task is to "install new bathroom suite" it is likely you will have to get the bath, basin, tiles, taps, shower, screen, toilet pan, seat, cistern and waste connectors. It would be impractical to try to include all that in a column on a spreadsheet or in any project management software. Let's be practical. The way we can include materials in a work plan is to have a column for associated documents. Each task would have a column to name the document or its path, which could be a hyperlink. The document to which the task points can be any type of document or a web page. It would include what the item is, including part numbers and from where you are most likely to procure it.

Now your plan is starting to take good shape: you know what skills you need or who could do the task and you have an idea of materials you may need to get hold of and have jotted down what you think the skills and / or materials will cost. There are two more things you need to include in your plan. You know what and who, but still need to fill the blanks for when and the estimated cost.

ESTIMATES IN YOUR WORK PLAN

Get an estimate from trades-people. Approach not only your preferred trades-person, but up to five others as well. Get their estimate of the size of each task (broken down if necessary), how long it is likely to take, what it will cost and when your trades can start. That is the number of days' actual work, the elapsed time it might take, the cost and when the particular individual/ firm is able to make a start. A three day task (e.g. plaster and paint) may take a couple of weeks to complete owing to the fact the plaster must dry out before decorating.

Look at the tasks and see which ones could be done by the same individual or business. Parcel up several tasks that are likely to require the same individual or business in order to refine your first thought on cost.

REQUEST ESTIMATES IN WRITING

Email or write to each trade outlining what work needs to be done (from the Scope document you prepared earlier) what materials you plan to source yourself, any specific colours, styles (taken from the mood board you may have prepared earlier) or professional standards you want and when your project is likely to be underway. This may be a simple cut and paste section of your Scope, a combination of elements from the Scope or the entire document, depending on what work you are trying to estimate. Explain the context and overall scope of the project.

In larger projects where you are dealing with larger firms rather than individuals you may be required to write up your requirements as a formal invitation to tender. I'll not dwell on the tender process here because if you are running a residential refurbishment project, the probability is that you will be working primarily with individuals or small businesses. Developments such as converting a building into several dwellings are more likely be put out to tender using a scoping document and / or a design specification.

Ask each potential trades-person if he/ she is interested in the work, how long they believe they would need to do the tasks and what they would estimate the cost to be. Ask if they would need to or like to do the work in one continuous run, or if they would recommend splitting it up, say three days one week and two days three weeks later. Ask when they are available and give them an idea of the dates you prefer.

Some trades-people such as sole traders may not be VAT registered whilst larger companies will be. This has an effect on cost. Just ask.

AN ESTIMATE IS NOT A QUOTE

At this point I guess I should remind you that an estimate is not a quote. An estimate is the time and cost required, *in their professional opinion,* in order to get the task done. What eventually happens and the actual cost may differ for a number of reasons. You are only asking for an estimate in order to plan the project and should make it clear that you can only come back to them to firm up on arrangements and price once you have consulted others involved in the project.

What I do at this point in my project planning is to take the average of the three costs and time estimates which best match my requirements. Matching my requirements will require some congruence with my vision of standards and when things are likely to happen. This is what I use to update my work plan.

Do bear in mind that project management software will be able to add up costs and time to do the work estimates for you automatically, rolling these up to give you figures for the higher task levels and the overall project. If you are using any paper method to plan your project you will have to do this manually. Arithmetic is not my strong hand, but for a very small project it may be no problem to add up a relatively small number of individual estimates.

ESTIMATING MATERIALS COSTS

Besides what you are going to have to pay for labour, there is the matter of materials. You have already identified what you think you will need. I say "think" because my experience shows me that there is always something I forget, which is why I always try to build a good relationship with suppliers and can ask them what else they think I might need. Good relationships with your suppliers makes for a stress free buying process, often with good discounts. Of course, there are also discount buying clubs and trade accounts available to you, as I have mentioned.

Armed with your documents and lists of materials needed, you can go out to several suppliers and ask what they can do for you. It is not only about price. Do they have the range you envisage? Do they give credit terms, so that you need not pay up front? Do they have what you want in stock? How long are the lead times? What are their returns policies? Do they charge for delivery? When do any promotional offers expire? Again I take the average of the most suitable three supplier prices for materials to input to my work plan in order to come up with a reasonable estimate for the cost. Just be reminded that software will add up the total materials costs for you, while paper will not.

What may be more critical for your project is timing. We are going to look at this in the section about "dependencies".

ALLOWANCES FOR CONTINGENCIES

Things will not go 100% according to plan. Something will always go wrong. That's life. Whether it is that some of your materials cost more than you thought, or that you had to replace someone at higher cost than anticipated, or that some tasks took longer than expected, the impact can be significant.

While you are planning your project you are managing the expectations of others involved in the project as well as yourself. If, for example, your lender is expecting to be repaid in six or twelve months then plan to meet such expectations. How? Allow 10 – 20% (as a rule of thumb) extra on both time and your budget. This is contingency. You have no intention of using that extra time or extra money, but if that is what you have told your stakeholders, then they will be pleasantly surprised when you complete the project in less time and / or at lower cost than predicted.

BIGGER PROJECTS – GREATER CONTINGENCY

The bigger the project the bigger the allowances for contingency. Although I have worked on much larger projects in the past, these days I am involved in residential refurbishment which is a much smaller type of project. So, for residential refurbishment, once you have the experience to be able to estimate fairly accurately (more of how that comes about later), I tend to put 10% contingency against both the estimated cost and the estimated end date. Where in the plan? I put in a separate item (that would be task to software) at the end. Including both time and cost contingencies allows you to communicate a worst case scenario. By including contingency within your plan, it enables you to delight your sponsors and partners, not to mention yourself, especially if you find there is no need to use that contingency.

Under promise and over deliver.

DEPENDENCIES WITHIN YOUR WORK PLAN

Remember TREAD carefully? D stands to remind you about dependencies.

We have nearly finished preparing a work plan for your refurbishment project. Now is the time to look at which task is dependent on which other task or tasks. Tasks need to be put into some sort of sequence. Intuitively you may have made a start, but let's consider a way to be more certain.

The dependencies in your work plan are the detail of what needs to have finished before something else can start. For example, you cannot start painting any walls that need to be plastered beforehand, so painting is dependent on the plastering having been completed. Don't forget you will also need some time between these tasks for the plaster to dry properly; this is called lag, but to keep it simple you can put in a task called something like "wait for plaster to dry". Apologies if that is obvious.

REWORK IS COSTLY

There are less obvious dependencies, such as one I witnessed when a building contractor had the gloss paintwork done beautifully in a couple of rooms that were almost finished; then he started hacking plaster off in a nearby room. The dust from that one room settled on the paint work in the other rooms and the painting had to be rubbed down and done again. Although I can't elaborate on his language, the air was a rather vivid shade. I haven't witnessed anything much more colourful than a building contractor furious with himself. It cost the poor chap in both his time and money, in terms of lost opportunity to get on with another job.

Rework is always costly, in terms of time, materials, labour and money.

If you are tempted to miss out the dependencies in your project plan, how can you truly say that you know what is going to happen and when? How can you be sure you will not have one tradesman standing around waiting for someone else to finish? How can you be certain when the project will come to successful conclusion?

If you do work out which tasks depend on something else, as well as which tasks can be done at the same time, side by side, then you will have the right people turning up at the right time, without hanging around, with every task that should have been done beforehand properly completed. If one task is taking longer than expected, dependent tasks may need to be delayed. You can see, from your plan, what and who needs to be rescheduled. You can save yourself time, money and sleepless nights by not having to rework those tasks.

FORGETTING DEPENDENCIES CAN BE EMBARRASSING

Not thinking about dependencies within your plan is rather like going out in the morning without getting dressed. Imagine getting up out of bed, doing everything you do in the bathroom and walking out of the house to pop over the road to pick up your daily paper. Imagine how red faced you might be when you arrive at the counter in whatever you sleep in (which might be just your skin)! With no clothes on, consequently no pockets, you may well have no money on you either.

So going to get a paper is dependent on you getting dressed and picking up sufficient money.

Once you have sprinted back to your home to get clothes and money, you need to rework the task of going to get a daily newspaper. OK, I hear you mutter, you can read the news on-line in the buff if you wish. However, I hope you can see the importance of thinking about dependencies in your work plan.

Rework is always costly and often embarrassing.

Although working out dependencies can be the most frustrating aspect of preparing your work plan, it is undoubtedly the step which, when done well, will save you so many headaches as the project progresses. The use of project management software tools makes this much easier, but you need to understand the process and reasoning first.

STEP BY STEP DEPENDENCIES – HOW TO

Let's take this step by step. Allocate each discreet task (the task with a duration of five days or less) a number. Project management software will do this for you, but if you are using a spreadsheet, make the task number the first column.

Now introduce a column for dependencies. In this column, against each task, enter the task number (or numbers) of every task that must be completed before this one can begin. The example that is coming up illustrates the principle.

Ask yourself the following questions:

- Can this task be done at the same time as another?
- What has to finish before this task can start?
- What other tasks cannot start until this task has finished?

Make a first pass at entering the number of each task upon which this one is dependent. Project management software will schedule the project dates to take into account all the dependencies you have entered and give you a time line. When you have done this first pass, ask yourself another question. Thinking back to when you spoke to each resource (trades-person) whose skills you planned to use, ask yourself are they going to be available when your plan suggests you need them? If not, when are they available? Adjust the dates accordingly. You may have to repeat this process several times, doing a reasonableness check each time.

Allow for a time delay (often referred to as lag) between ordering materials and delivery exactly as you did for the situation where you had to wait for plaster to dry. Alternatively you can add a task called something like “awaiting delivery”.

THE GANTT CHART - CRITICAL PATH

Once you are happy with the dependencies you will be able to produce a diagram of the timeline and see the critical path; that is the longest sequence of tasks that *must* follow one another to complete the project. This is a Gantt chart. Most project management software produces this for you automatically, saving you hours of hard and demanding mental work. It doesn’t have to be MsProject. There are several other project management software products that you can try out for free, such as www.smartsheet.com or www.openproject.org.

A simple Gantt chart might look something like the following illustration. We can learn a lot from it, just as an example. The example project has only five tasks and is expected to last four months. Real projects have more tasks, but there are always dependencies. As you can see, we can show quite a lot of important information using a chart.

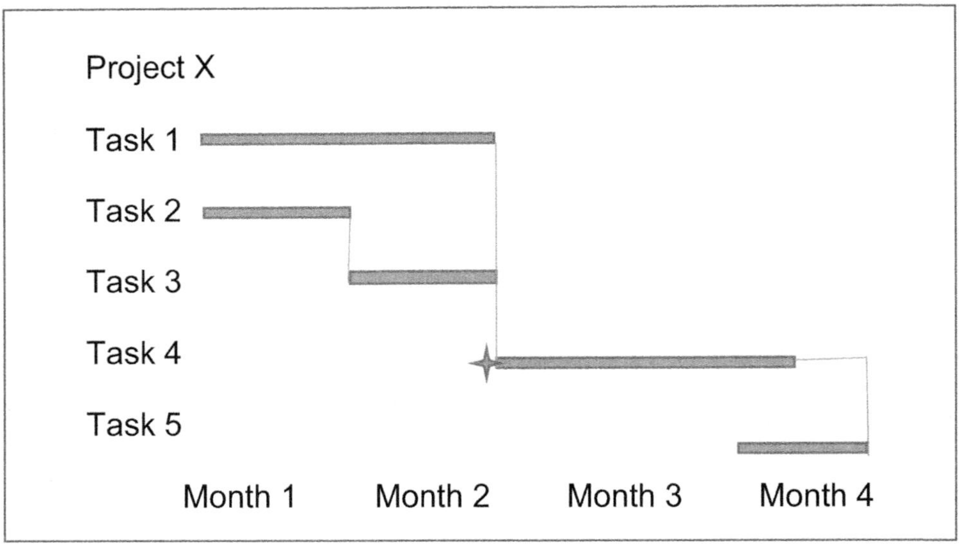

All the tasks are listed on the left and the dates for your project are shown along the bottom to give you a timeline. Whether you decide to use days, weeks, months or even quarters is up to you and who you are trying to inform with your Gantt chart.

From this example we can see the following main points.

- Tasks one and two can start on the same date, although they are not expected to take the same amount of time.
- Task three cannot start until we have completed task two.
- Task four cannot start until we have completed both task one and task three.
- Task five can start at any time as there is no previous task upon which it is dependent.
- Task five can only be completed once task four has been completed.

IT IS A PEOPLE BUSINESS

I'm sure you will have heard criticisms before about how decisions have been taken without letting anyone know. Never forget that project management and property are both people businesses and people like to know how things are going. Now, if your project is going to take more than just a few months, may I suggest you introduce something to help from two very important perspectives?

- Reassurance for sponsors / Joint Venture partners
- Morale within the team

So what am I talking about? I'll tell you. I'm talking about milestones. That is what that little star is in the example chart earlier.

MILESTONES

If a project is being undertaken in phases, it is easy to see where to take a step back, review, reward the team and make decisions. Use a milestone at the end of each phase e.g. after finishing one flat of what may be a block of four flats.

A milestone at the end of each main group of tasks can be really helpful. A key point in time, or milestone, is where people are involved to decide whether or not to proceed with later phases or stages of a project. You can have a milestone where ever you choose, as in our example just before we start task four. We need milestones to evaluate whether or not we are going to succeed or fail and what we need to do to succeed. We will look at how to evaluate the situation at a later stage.

People stop to make decisions at milestones.

SPONSORS AND PARTNERS LOVE MILESTONES

Sponsors and partners will, almost certainly, want to know how the project is progressing and when it reaches specific points, or milestones, along the way. Agree which tasks are a milestone with them. Mark the relevant task as a milestone. When it is reached, tell the sponsors and partners the good news. If you think you will miss one, tell them the bad news too. People like to be respected and kept in the picture. That way, they can be confident that the project is being properly managed and know where their money is being spent. Milestones offer a means within the project for reassurance.

MILESTONES MOTIVATE

The team of workers on any project can become despondent if they can see no end in sight. Milestones are there so that everyone can see where the project is going to be and exactly when. They can see when each important point will be reached. It is motivating to have a target that can be visualised and is not too far away. Once you have the project work plan completed, all members of the team can see where they fit into the overall picture and where the key decision points will be. Milestones offer a mechanism within the project work plan by which success can be measured and rewarded, but more of rewarding later.

A FINAL WORD ABOUT YOUR WORK PLAN

Follow this framework and you will have *a clearly documented work plan*, complete with **T**asks, **R**esources, **E**stimates, **A**llowance for contingencies and **D**ependencies. Make it available to everyone involved in the project. Some may not read it, but you can only lead a horse to water; you cannot make it drink (or read your work plan).

If you measure success in terms of getting the project done on time, with it costing much as you predicted and to your predefined standard, then you must make a plan. Many who have managed projects without planning, regardless of whether or not that was a property project, will have failed either to meet their timescale, to stay within budget or to end up with what they intended. It isn't worth the risk; you need to make a documented plan.

Key points to remember
• Fail to plan and you plan to fail • Rework is always costly. Do tasks in the right order • Make a start, with an outline and your best estimates • Each detail task should last no more than five days • Different skills incur different costs for a day • Allow 10% to 20% contingency on time and budget • Under promise and over deliver • Milestones motivate and offer reassurance

CHAPTER 7 PLAN - BUDGET & STAKEHOLDERS

A BUDGET PLAN

I do not intend to go on about budgeting in *all* its forms. All I'll say is that if you do not have a decent budget plan, documented for others involved in the project to see, you are likely to spend more than you anticipated and make sponsors and the like somewhat nervous. That's an under-statement.

Just imagine going on holiday for a couple of weeks with no idea of how much you expect to spend and then relying on your credit card for day to day expenses. It can soon mount up, can't it? Have you ever, I wonder, returned home and had a shock when you got your statement showing how much you'd spent. Now if you had thought it through, had a holiday project plan and planned to spend only up to a certain limit each day, you could check your account periodically and know when to make adjustments and not face debt on returning.

Your budget plan is the third of the main elements of the project which you need to document in some form or another.

FIRM UP WITH QUOTES

Once you have a work plan, you can go back to those estimates which you pulled together earlier on. Some trades will have given you a quote right there and then, while others will have given you an estimate based on a rough idea of how many days are required and when they are needed. With the work plan ready, you do need to go back to each person involved and ask them just two things.

- Their availability on the dates that have come out of your work plan
- Their quote for the work, now that they can see the overall picture

A fixed price may cost a little more, but is often more controllable than an estimated number of days and a man day rate. Be careful to refer to your Scope document and do not take on any extra tasks. Extra tasks cost money. You can now refine the costs in the work plan using the quotes.

Treat materials in exactly the same way as you have just done for the human resources. Check availability against your timeline and get a firm quote from suppliers. Only by doing this can you choose which suppliers to buy from so that orders can be placed as soon as the project is ready to make a start.

Project management software will show you what you are about to spend and when, provided you have entered all the details correctly.

CASH FLOW FORECAST

What I like to do in order to be able to keep track of my spending and communicate to sponsors what is being spent, is to use a spreadsheet to prepare a simple cash flow forecast. To me this is part of the process of budgeting for the project. In, say, a 12 month project, a cash flow forecast provides me with a prediction of how much money I will need on a month by month basis. Until you have a work plan, with its timeline (Gantt chart) in place you are not in a position to plan out the month by month expenditure (and income perhaps). Investors always want to know where the money is going and when they can expect to see a return on their investment.

Using spreadsheet software or a sheet of paper (if it is a short project and you are good at mental arithmetic – I'm not), put the months of your project across into the columns. Then enter the tasks that incur cost into the rows. I always put the cost of materials close to the task for ordering them unless I have agreed delayed payment terms. It is then simply a matter of referring to your work plan, taking the costs from there and inserting the costs against each task in the appropriate cash flow column for the month you expect to have to pay it out. Then sum the columns to give a figure for the each month. Now sum the costs in the rows to give a figure for each task.

Referring to the milestones in your work plan, considered against the cash flow forecast, you can quickly see how much you had expected to spend by the time you reach each milestone / key decision point. This gives you something to work towards and against which to test your progress later so that everyone involved can be kept in the picture. It is not unusual for an investor/ landlord to run out of money before the final fittings are in place, simply because he / she did not prepare a cash flow forecast and over spent on earlier tasks.

CASH FLOW EXAMPLE

Remember the Gantt chart for Project X in the last chapter? Let's consider how the cash might flow.

Project X						**Totals**
Expenditure	**Mth 1**	**Mth 2**	**Mth 3**	**Mth4**	**Proj. End**	
Task 1	800		700			**1,500**
Task 2	230	75				305
Task 3			850			850
Task 4				750	295	1,045
Task 5				850	850	1,700
Contingency					540	540
Income			-2500		-2500	-5000
Month Total	**1,030**	**75**	**-950**	**1,600**	**-815**	**940**

I initially prepared this in Excel, so I let the software do the arithmetic. That was much easier than getting it into text. Income is shown as minus, by convention. You can see the costs associated to each task in the right hand column. Let me explain the example.

In this simple illustration we have a sponsor who has agreed to contribute £2,500 at the beginning of month three, once the milestone has been reached satisfactorily. The sponsor has also agreed to contribute another £2,500 once the project is complete.

For each of tasks one and two you can see that we have to find some money up front and the rest is due once the task is completed. Task three is being paid for only when it is finished. The contractor undertaking task four is willing to make a start and take an interim payment, with the final payment being made once task five has completed as he is doing task five as well. Payment for task five will be made with the final payment for task four.

I have allowed 10% of the sum of the tasks for contingency at the end.

The sponsor's contributions are shown against expected income, using a minus figure to gauge how much of our own money we will need and, most importantly, when. Looking at the bottom row (totals for each month) you can see that we need 1,030 to get the project under way. We also need a further 75 at the start of month two. Once our sponsor has paid us 2,500 and we get to the start of month three we will have 950 in the bank. Take your time to understand what the cash flow forecast is telling you.

By the time we reach the end of the project, it will have used up 940 of our own money, that is if we had to use all the contingency. If we were spot on with our estimates and had no need to use any contingency we would have used up only 400 of our own money.

A COMMUNICATIONS PLAN

Besides the scope, the work plan and the cash flow outlined earlier, you need to plan how to communicate with all interested parties. Why? Well, how would you feel if you had invested in a project and never knew when or how to find out about its progress? I hate being kept in the dark. It is the one thing during a project that really makes my hackles rise.

PLAN TO AVOID CONFLICT

How would you feel if you had no idea who else you may have to be working with? I can remember having an electrician who thought my heating engineer was "rubbish" and the heating engineer told me he would never work on a place which "that electrician" has bodged up. Both felt passionately. So, I never hire both of them on the same project. Both electrician and heating engineer know from my communications plan who they will be working with; it avoids friction. That's why you need a plan for how you are going to communicate with sponsors, joint venture partners, contractors and others involved in the project.

On larger projects the communications plan is likely to include the work plan. On smaller projects an outline plan with key milestones is often sufficient. This tells everyone what is expected to happen and when.

PLAN TO KEEP EVERYONE IN TOUCH

Who are the stakeholders? Who is working on the project? The communications plan is there to answers these questions.

The key component of the communications plan, which is found nowhere else in the planning documents, is when and how progress is going to be reported and to whom.

Who are you going to be providing with progress reports? On larger projects there may well be a project board or steering group made up of key stakeholders and representatives from the customers. On our residential property refurbishments, it is our joint venture partners and you, yourself, to whom progress has to be reported. If you have borrowed money, or need money to be drawn down at key milestone points, then you must report progress regularly and consistently (there is that word again).

When and how will you be getting progress reports? Are you going to ask trades to fill in a time sheet? Some folk would. I wouldn't, unless we are carrying out a large project over a significant period of time. I would, however, include in the communications plan the fact that progress is going to be monitored weekly, but that any problems will be reported to me by email or text as soon as they emerge. Do you agree that it is often good to have some sort of predictability and routine? You may not, but I believe it helps to know that progress is going to be checked on a specific day of each week and state so in the plan. If you intend to get key trades or your stakeholders together (perhaps once a month) for a face to face meeting to see how the project is progressing, then state so in the communications plan. State who, where and when.

SPECIFICS IN THE COMMUNICATIONS PLAN

Put somewhat simply, the communications plan must include the following specifics:

- key milestones (decision points)
- when progress is going to be checked and how often
- a list of contact names
- email addresses and phone numbers

Just make sure all players in your project give written consent to share their contact details and that they each have a copy.

Once the planning has been done and documented, wouldn't you agree that the whole project is coming into much clearer focus? Planning is by far the biggest element of the investor / landlord project manager's role.

Before we move on to the second stage, there are just a couple of points I want to mention: risk and people.

A WORD ABOUT RISK

Let's not forget risks to the success of your project. Risk is often about health and safety. Yet it can also encompass money and resources, all of which have an impact on people.

Remember the health and safety of those who will live in your property. I have mentioned that UK law puts a duty of care on you to ensure that the property is fit for people to live in at the beginning of any tenancy. Electrical and gas safety are crucial. Insulation and the energy performance of the property are equally important. It is important to *plan* the tasks and budget for health and safety compliance.

Safety during the project cannot be ignored either. A wise project manager will prepare a risk assessment. Greater detail is available from the Health & Safety Executive (HSE) and the National Landlords Association (NLA). Just make sure it is communicated to everyone contributing to any work on the project. You are responsible for the welfare of everyone working on your project or, indeed, visiting the site. More on this in the next chapter.

A WORD ABOUT PEOPLE

At this point, having a sound power team in place will be enormously beneficial. It takes time. Building your power team of professionals for each geographical area in which you plan to invest is all part of the business planning and set up process. In an ideal world, building a team comes before or at the very start of the project, while you are planning all the other things. Life often differs from the ideal world and if you have just inherited the property you need to refurbish, for example, then you need to sort out a team right now.

It helps to get to know each person you are planning to work with. It helps to know how they work, such as their lead time; that is how far ahead they plan their work.

For example, in the Medway area, where most of my refurbishments take place, I have built a good relationship with my heating and plumbing engineer, so can generally expect to be able to get him to fit in my jobs within a few days of my contacting him. The electrician, another key member of the team with whom I have a good relationship, needs a good two or three weeks' advance notice. If I order a new kitchen it can take anything from two days to two months before delivery, depending on how bespoke or otherwise the specification and what is available from stock. It helps to use the same supplier all the while you are happy with their products. Get to know the warehouse people too as well as how and when they get deliveries.

Who is in the team? Although I shall not dwell on this here, because this is more about how to build a property business, the *key people* are likely to include:

- A solicitor
- An accountant

- An architect
- A plasterer
- A painter / decorator
- An electrician
- A plumber
- A kitchen fitter

It helps to have a good understanding of what needs to be done and in what sequence. You did your best to get this right whilst preparing the work plan.

ORDERING MATERIALS FROM SUPPLIERS

Now you can order materials at the right time and get your team lined up while you tidy up and refine your plan.

Think about where you may be able to get a good discount. Suppliers with whom you build a good working relationship will subsequently become members of your power team. Then there are discount buying clubs such as the Landlords National Property Group, although several of the larger builders' merchants also offer discounts for promised repeat business.

As part of the plan you will need to take into account how long you may have to wait between ordering and taking delivery of materials to fit in with anticipated availability of key trades in the geographical area in which you are working. When you have to chase up suppliers, remember to continue building that relationship.

You need to get organised. Remember, you want to maximise profit and minimise wasted time and / or money.

Planning is the first stage in the project process. It is now time for the second stage where we **U**nleash the work force.

Key points to remember
• Get firm quotes for work • Ask for discounts from suppliers • Prepare a cash flow forecast • Plan to communicate and be consistent • Consider project risks • Maximise profit, minimise wasted time and / or money • Develop good relationships with suppliers and trades

CHAPTER 8 UNLEASH THE WORK FORCE

I wonder how you might feel if you decided to do almost everything yourself, including:

- procurement (finding and ordering materials)
- building work
- carpentry
- electrical and gas work
- painting and decorating
- negotiations with local authorities for planning / building regulations (a requirement for work that does anything to the fabric or external look of the building)
- site clearance

My guess is you might be shattered, even if you did have all the requisite skills.

On the other hand, if you just potter along without even a plan, hiring people as the mood takes you, the project might take a very long time, during which there may be loan payments to be met or partners to be rewarded. It could feel like living in the jaws of hell. JAWS is the acronym I use to help me remember what to do during the second stage of any project.

This is when we unleash the workforce and think of Jaws.

So, what does JAWS remind me of?

- **J**ob Sheet
- **A**uthorise your workforce
- **W**elfare of your workforce
- **S**tandards required of your workforce

MANY HANDS MAKE LIGHT WORK

You are almost sure to have heard the saying "many hands make light work". If you can get several *appropriate* people to work on your project instead of doing everything yourself, imagine how much more quickly you are likely to finish. To manage several tradespeople at the same time requires good planning. This is what you have been working towards. With a plan in place you now need to get the work done. If you don't, then all that effort has been a waste of time (unless it was an academic exercise). When you do start to get the work done, the project is well and truly underway, with visible results.

MOBILISE THE WORKFORCE

Now, if you have enlisted the right trades and professionals and planned how they will interact, you've a good idea of who should be doing what, when and how. Having several pairs of hands in the right place at the right time can save you weeks or months, save your money and enable you to market the property without undue delay. Bear in mind that the tradespeople from your power team, to whom you talked during the planning stage, may not be available to your time table. Be prepared to find yourself in a position where you may occasionally have to find someone else. If you do I'd suggest there are a few ways to find those fall back tradespeople.

- Recommendations are the best way to find an alternative tradesperson when you have to. Ask other property people, such as other investors, estate or letting agents who they might recommend.
- Find reliable trades in your Parish magazine or on websites such as Checkatrade or RatedPeople. Read the reviews and any testimonials.
- When you see work being done on properties nearby, talk to the workmen / women and ask if they can help, either directly or by putting you in touch with someone they trust.

Qualify prospective trades and get information about their previous track record, perhaps going to see work they have previously carried out. Other things to check include:

- Availability
- Qualifications
- Where they mostly work. If they work in Dartford they may not need work in Tonbridge
- Do they let you have a landline number as well as a mobile number

- Do they have a website? Check whois.com to see who owns the business website
- Do they reveal their address?
- What insurance cover do they have in place?
- Size of jobs previously undertaken
- VAT registration status
- How they prefer to be paid

In order to give yourself the best chance of finding a suitable contractor, meet with three to six who sound promising. You can approach more (say ten) on a large development project, but a development project is outside the scope of this guide. Chat about the job and listen; listen to get a feel for whether or not they know what they are doing. The more experience you gain in your property refurbishments, the easier it becomes for you to spot a cowboy or inexperienced individual or firm. When you have found someone you can work with, ask for a written quote of both cost and timing.

QUALIFYING TRADES

Filter out the ones you decide not to use. There are many reasons for your decision, just a few of which I'll mention here.

- Not everyone you ask or try to meet will get back to you. They may be too busy and not need new work. You cannot wait for those people if your project is to keep going in a timely fashion.

- Beware of anyone who tells you they can do anything and everything. Remember Jack of all trades and master of none?
- Beware of anyone who likes to work on the job alone when you are not likely to be about. On two occasions I have fallen foul of this. In each case the job was done too slowly and certainly not how I wanted it done. Learn from my experience and save yourself time and distress.
- The cheapest quote is not necessarily the most suitable, but it is up to you to decide which, if any, you wish to accept. Before making a decision, consider why a particular quote is cheaper than the rest.

Accept in writing (email is fine) clearly indicating *what* you are accepting. For those who quoted but you did not accept, decline politely in writing in order to leave the door open in case you need them in the future.

BE VERY AWARE OF HEALTH AND SAFETY

As I may have mentioned earlier, two main sets of regulatory guidelines exert an influence over how you run your project. You do need to be very aware of health and safety right from the planning stage, throughout the refurbishment and as you come to complete your projects. The regulatory guidelines are:

- CDM (construction, design and management) which applies during refurbishment or development
- HHSRS (Housing Health and Safety Rating System) which applies to the finished property

CDM

Since 2015 refurbishment projects on *any* property, other than your own home, need to be run using the guidelines embedded in CDM – construction, design, management - where health and safety are embedded as the foundation for safe working.

Even on a small refurbishment, someone, and it may be you, has to accept responsibility for the health and safety of anyone whilst they are working on your project. That individual holds the role of CDM Manager. Don't get carried away by this important sounding title. Use common sense. Stay safe and keep anyone who visits the project site safe too. I make no claim to be an expert on health and safety, so consult the Health and Safety Executive. Look up www.hse.gov.uk. This is the quickest and easiest way to get on the right track.

A written project risk assessment is your best starting point. I recommend you prepare one using a pro forma such as that on the HSE website.

If your project is big enough, e.g. a major refurbishment requiring structural work for which you will have obtained the necessary building regulation consents, you may be putting the project out to a main contractor. A main contractor should have the appropriate knowledge (and qualifications) of CDM to undertake the key role of CDM manager. However, be careful to have a *written* agreement regarding who takes on this, and other roles, for compliance. It may be you as overall project manager. Build this role into your work plan.

Be clear at the outset whether you are hiring a lead contractor who will organise the whole job and check for competence, or if it is up to you to hire individual trades at the appropriate times. Be clear as to who is responsible for liability insurance. Check whether or not you already have the necessary insurance cover with a reputable broker if in doubt.

HHSRS

Standing for Housing Health and Safety Rating System, this is the set of standards and guidelines for the finished product - a safe and healthy home for someone. As we have already mentioned, there will be many tasks built into the work plan to ensure compliance and to ensure you can provide a decent home for decent people. The NLA website has a whole training module on HHSRS; I suggest you take a look at it.

SIMPLIFYING THE PROCESS

For most residential property refurbishment projects, although some paper work is necessary, I like to simplify matters and use what I already have. Does that sound OK with you?

In my project process, I use the acronym JAWS at this stage. This is the second stage, remember, as I mentioned in the last chapter. It serves to remind me what to do, in order to unleash the work force (professionals, me and trades) onto the project. It concentrates our efforts by making use of any paperwork we already have and avoids any unnecessary documentation.

Remember what JAWS stands for? No? Go back half a dozen pages or let me recap.

- **J**ob Sheet
- **A**uthorise
- **W**elfare
- **S**tandards

We can look at each of these steps in turn.

JOB SHEET

This can be a form, email, letter or specification, depending on your style and project size. On a larger project, where you are hiring a main contractor to bring it all together on your behalf, you would be more likely to call this a Design Specification. The information included is fundamentally the same information and can be partially assembled from documents you already have from the planning stage.

It is important to explain exactly:

- what needs to be done
- when you expect it to start
- when you expect it to finish

- what you expect it to cost
- how you are going to pay
- who is supplying materials
- the standard of finish you require.

This all sounds simple enough doesn't it? The more precise you can be, the less the risk of misunderstandings and disappointment.

USE WHAT YOU ALREADY HAVE

To avoid unnecessary paperwork, make up the job sheet (or pack) from what you already have. You have an email or letter with the quote and your written acceptance. Use it. Include other information from your planning, which ought to include:

- The work plan, or at least that part of it which shows tasks upon which this job is dependent and tasks dependent upon completion of this job
- Mood boards, colour samples
- Details of the materials you will provide and what the contractor needs to provide, along with a clear agreement regarding whether or not the contractor has included the cost for materials in his quote
- Paint and fabric samples if you require a specific finish
- How many coats of paint you expect where you are using a decorator

- Drawings, some of which you can get from a kitchen or bedroom designer
- Details of who is responsible for clearing rubbish away or recycling afterwards
- How and when you will meet to communicate progress

Sometimes being precise in writing is not enough, as I have learned from past bitter experience. It is not that people can't read, it is more that they are sure they know what you want and just want to get on with it and get paid soonest. It can save rework and time if you go through the job sheet pack / design specification with the contractor at the point of starting their particular job. Talk them through the pack. Pointing (yes, I use a pencil to actually point) to salient aspects of the drawings helps focus attention somewhat. Sticking drawings up on the wall, which I tend to do, *can* also help, but no guarantees.

WHY WOULD SOMEONE IGNORE THE DRAWINGS?

I once had a kitchen fitter to whom I gave detailed drawings and artist's impressions showing where everything was to go and where every electrical socket and connection was to be installed. The electrician followed the drawings. The fitter ignored them and cut a hole (a huge irregular shape, to make matters worse) in the back of one of my new kitchen base units. When you ask "why" try not to shriek as I may have done on that occasion. His reply was that he *assumed* I wanted to connect the hob to the previously disconnected power supply. This was despite the fact it didn't meet current regulations, had been terminated and was some four metres away from where the new hob should go. Everything was clearly shown on the drawing and there was a new supply point in place ready for the new hob. He didn't look at the drawings as he "knew what the layout should be". That one hole cost the fitter his weekend to put matters right, not to mention the cost to him of replacing the damaged unit back. Hopefully he learned the lesson that rework is costly.

AUTHORISE

Step back and authorise the people you have hired to get on with the job. Step back from the detail but be there to support. They know their profession better than you. Unless you are qualified, for example, to rewire a property, keep out of the way while a qualified electrician does the work. When managing your project just make sure the electrician, for example, has the materials, a clear job description, the space and environment he needs. Give him the authority to go ahead but be prepared and available to answer questions as detailed points arise. By all means be on site and on hand to answer queries; just don't hover!

Let your workforce know where you will be working while they are on the premises and tell them you are there for their health and safety. If they have an accident you can administer first aid, call an ambulance or drive them to A&E. You'll almost never need to help in this way, but give them the message that you are there for their safety and that you will not be getting under their feet or telling them how to do their job.

RESPECT

Respect the skills each member of your team has. It is OK to ask about what is happening and why, but do so in the spirit of learning, not judging. Apologise for perhaps using the wrong terms and ask what you should call something. Actively demonstrate that you respect the fact that your skilled contractor knows more about the detail of a task than you do; regulations change over time and it is the skilled tradesman who keeps abreast of regulatory updates, not necessarily you.

WELFARE

Property is a people business, as I suspect you have come to appreciate. I cannot emphasise this point too strongly. If you already have good people skills, residential property projects are going to become more successful. Look after your people. Happy workers are productive workers. Grumpy workers seldom get the job done and almost never go that extra mile to get your job done on time.

It is up to you to consider your own welfare and that of the other workers, during the refurbishment. Common sense really? As investor / landlord professionals who refurbish property and act as

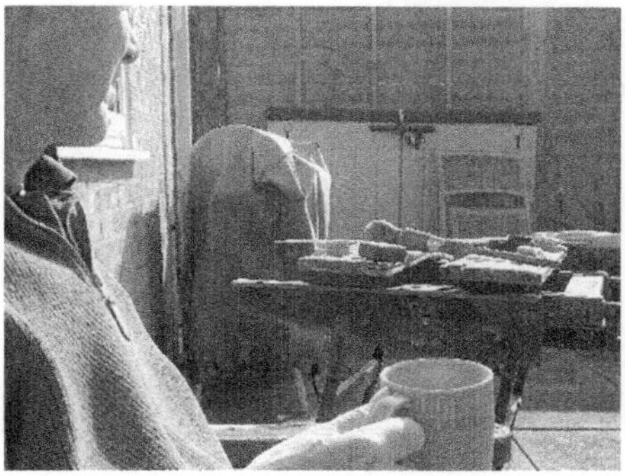

project managers, it is you and I who have a moral duty of care to each member of the work force. When hiring others to do the work we must look after their welfare. I'll share with you the sort of things I do to keep happy workers who are willing to work with me again.

- Provide somewhere for your workers to sit down and have a cup of tea / coffee
- Get in squash or fruit juice if you ever have an electrician changing the consumer unit/s as you will have no power to boil a kettle for several hours, a day or longer, depending on the scale of the project
- Somewhere (civilised) to go to the loo, making sure there is sufficient toilet paper and anti-bacterial hand cleanser, with a hot water tap accessible
- Find out what they like to be called. One of my preferred contractors is a carpenter called William who likes to be called Will, not Bill or William. Speak to people by name. You might be surprised at how important, however sub conscious it might be, to address someone by the name they prefer
- Somewhere to shelter when the weather turns too bad
- On a larger site, somewhere to dry wet clothes and securely store PPE (personal protective equipment such as wet weather gear and hard hats)

- Consider providing biscuits, sweets or even favourite butties. One of the best ground works teams I know run on bacon sandwiches
- Be a person of your word
- Avoid stressing people out by changing your mind. This is why you prepared a written statement of the scope of the project earlier on
- Arrange liability insurance appropriate to the situation, dependent on whether or not someone other than you is the lead contractor
- Encourage the workers to take a half hour minimum break for lunch. They will be far more effective. Chat to them over short (I mean short, you don't want to stop them working too long) tea breaks; it helps them see you as human
- Agree up front how you are going to pay for the work and pay promptly. Pay up on time once you have the invoice, not a week later

What, you may ask, will encourage someone to want to work with you rather than someone else?

In a nutshell, *look after your workforce, stay within scope and pay promptly.*

STANDARDS

Make the required standard is clear from the beginning. I've already mentioned the type, brand and number of coats of paint. This is part of the job pack. Talking it through (as well) with everyone involved always helps. Ask for alternative opinions. If the job involves brick laying, plastering, or decorating it is quite customary to get each person who is doing the job to do a sample section, or ask them how they intend going about it. Alternatively you can visit previous work or look at photos of actual recent jobs to see the standard of workmanship.

The steps of the project process I have learned from the puma and my past experience are all interdependent, none more so than the standard and quality of the work carried out by the work force. The resources, time and cost estimates you used when you prepared the work plan are a reflection of the standard expected of people working on the project. Make sure everyone understands what you expect *before* the work starts.

Many Quality Hands Make Light Work.

BEWARE PROJECT CREEP

Don't panic. Stay focussed. The written statement of the scope of the project which you prepared at the outset, will help you stay focussed.

Many a project has overrun either time wise, budget wise or both, because of what we tend to call "project creep". Project creep occurs when you (or your client / sponsors) change your/ their minds part way through about what you want the end to look like. Remember Stephen Covey's advice to start with the end in mind.

Don't only start, *keep* the end in mind. Focus on what you stated was within in the scope of the project (unless you have formally agreed to a change and the consequent difference in time and cost). Do not allow the project to drag on because someone suggests it might be "nice" to just have something else or use different materials. Formally agreeing a change in scope, with the associated time and cost implications needs to be a previously agreed procedure (that's change management which is a subject by itself and outside the scope of this guide). This tends to be used on large projects, rather than on a simple single unit refurbishment.

THINK OF THE DOG

By now I suspect you have started to think about *how* you can get the job done and keep everyone safe and happy, once you have unleashed them? Many dog owners (not unlike project managers in many respects) can get a bit stressed the first time they let their best friend off the lead and see him dash off after the first rabbit or sheep he smells. Would you agree that to turn your back on your dog at that point could end in disaster?

A friend and I had a near disaster, when her water loving dog unexpectedly jumped into a fast flowing, steep sided stream and couldn't get out with the stick she had proudly found and would not let go of. Someone had to help get her out. We got quite wet. You need a series of commands, gestures, whistles, rewards and sometimes muscle and cunning to recover your dog before he/ she gets into trouble or upsets the local farmer or worse, drowns.

EXPECT THE UNEXPECTED

It is much the same with a team working on a refurbishment project. You plan. You unleash the workforce. Someone may go off at a tangent (chasing rabbits). You need to keep an eye on what happens next; it may not be what you planned. Accidents happen.

Stay focussed, but expect the unexpected.

With the workforce unleashed, it's up to you to think how you can keep an eye on the timing, costs and the standard being achieved and keep everything clear of disasters?

You may be wondering what I am talking about. I'm talking about monitoring project progress against the work plan that you put so much effort into at the start of the project.

Key points to remember
• Many quality hands make light work • Beware Jack of all trades / master of none • Speak to (and of) people by name - the one they prefer to be called • Respect professional knowhow and don't hover • Have a job sheet / pack / specification before work starts • Make sure people read the instructions to the end • Happy workers are productive workers • Stay within the scope, look after the workers and pay promptly, i.e. don't humbug anyone about • Stay focussed but expect the unexpected

CHAPTER 9 MONITOR

Let's have a recap on the overall process for managing your refurbishment project, before we go on. As you remember I rely on the PUMA to remind me of the fundamental four stages.

- **Pl**an
- **U**nleash the workforce
- **M**onitor
- **A**nalyse

At this stage of any project, your job as the person overseeing or managing the project, is to keep an eye on how things are going. Sounds easy, doesn't it? It is a simple process, but what is less easy is making sure everyone is working well together and they have what they need when they need it.

Simple is not necessarily easy.

All that time and effort you put into planning the work and budget for the project will pay off, making this stage of the project much more straightforward.

Perhaps I should introduce the idea of a Project Manager's day book here. You may call it a note book. Much depends on the formality of the project. Regardless of what you call it, you need a book (or notepad / iPad), for each project, in which to keep all your notes, especially those you make as you monitor progress. Simple rules I'd never do without are, start a new page per date and note down everything.

Rather like a detective with his cape DRAPEd about his shoulders, pipe in hand and probing questions (remind you of anyone?) you need to be curious, persistent and consistent in monitoring / investigating progress.

Be curious, persistent and consistent.

DRAPE reminds me of the five steps of the monitoring stage.

- **D**elegation
- **R**eporting
- **A**ctuals
- **P**roblems
- **E**stimate to go

Keep an eye on how things are going, without coming across as an officious clip board man (or woman). You'll need to use all your senses and skills to detect something which might be going anything other than perfectly according to plan.

DELEGATION NOT ABDICATION

Abdication is simply giving out the work and expecting it to be done on time, within budget and to your standard without keeping an eye on how it is going. *Abdication* is handing out enough rope for the workforce to hang themselves; this is not likely to get the project completed on time, if at all.

Delegation means giving the professional enough freedom to do the work while you retain responsibility, keep an eye on work progress, any issues arising and on the welfare of the people involved. It is not about you doing all the work yourself, but, instead, about you keeping an eye on progress and making sure everything is in place, all the time, thus enabling others to get on with the tasks and complete them on time, within your budget and to the requisite standard.

Years ago, when I first started out managing projects, I found it difficult to fully appreciate the difference between delegation and abdication. It is costly. It never ceases to surprise me how many people misunderstand what is expected of them. Could it be that the direction given by the manager was not completely clear? I have said it earlier, and I'll say it again, walk through drawings and instructions on the job sheet with the person who is doing the work, at the outset. Even doing this is not fool proof. You will still need to monitor on a regular basis even after responsibility for the work has been delegated.

REPORTING

Reporting is essential, but I avoid using the word when talking with any tradespeople. Be careful. Crucially, beware of certain psychological blocks. An unusually large number of both skilled and manual workers go peculiarly defensive at the word "reporting". Avoid said word (reporting) when near anyone doing physical work on your project. It is not the word itself which is the issue, but the psychological reaction to it.

It is important you remain focussed on what is happening. You've heard this before, but it is up to you and only you to be consistent and persistent. It's up to you to make progress meetings happen and remind everyone involved in the project when you want to meet. Make sure you do meet with key people week in, week out, no matter how weary you may feel or what else is happening in your life. Avoid distractions. Be aware if anyone is running behind, if anything has gone wrong or if anything looks likely to drag on or go wrong. Failure to keep your eye on the ball can be costly, especially if that holds up the next few dependent tasks.

WHY REPORT REGULARLY

I'll give you an example of why regular reporting is necessary. Suppose you have a waste pipe or gas pipe running across the wall behind where you are planning to fit a built in oven or washing machine. The oven or washing machine *may* not fit back far enough into the space. Measure up before work starts. If you do not spot the pipe when the old cupboards came out, before the fitter comes to connect up the appliances, then you may have to stop at the last minute and figure out a solution. It is far better to have issues reported as soon as they appear.

There are wide worktops available on the market, but these tend to be non-standard and may not be readily available from stock. Having to send the fitter away whilst you think of a solution (wider worktops or relocating appliances), getting a carpenter (at a cost) to re-arrange part of the fixtures and then rearranging for the fitter to return (more cost) at a later date, will mean delays after delays. It will also cost more than the original plan. It may also mean that your flooring contractor cannot lay the flooring when planned, which could be a significant delay as flooring people, it seems to me, are always heavily booked up and tend to dislike change immensely. By simply using your eyes and looking around your site you should spot issues such as the wayward pipework early on. Can you see how not monitoring how the project is developing can hinder the prospects of your ultimate success?

Seemingly small details, when overlooked, lead to big headaches. Avoid headaches: keep an eye on the detail.

AVOID OVERKILL

If you follow a few simple guidelines, use reporting sensibly (avoiding overkill) and adjust your attitude to differing groups of people, you will have increased the likelihood of bringing in your project on time, within budget, to your standard and keep people happy to work with you again. So, there are two directions of reporting, up and down. There are also two groups of people you need to report to, stakeholders and workers. Let's look at them in turn.

- The project manager (you) reports to the stakeholders (JV partners, whoever hired you or yourself)
- The project manager (you) reports to the workers, for want of a better expression
- The workers (plumbers, carpenters, fitters, painters etc.) report to you
- The stakeholders (JV partners, the bank, and (yes) yourself) report to you. Don't try and kid yourself

At least one of those may seem odd to you, but bear with me.

REPORTING TO STAKEHOLDERS

When *you report to stakeholders* your approach is going to be either informal or formal. Whichever approach you use, it makes you accountable. Accountability matters.

First, let's consider informal reporting. When you are working alone for your own project and funding it yourself, I strongly advise you to have someone else around, such as your significant other or a friend who is interested in your project. For this type of informal method of reporting, I advise making a habit of regularly (perhaps weekly) meeting over coffee, having a 'phone or Skype call (or similar) simply to let someone else know if you are on track, over or under budget (no-one else need know the figures) and on time or running late.

Now, if you have been hired by someone else, or if a JV partner is footing the bill whilst you are managing the project, you do need to be more formal. On large projects it is not unusual to have to prepare something in writing to a Project Board. On small to medium sized projects you may be reporting to a handful of individuals. Regardless of the size of the project, stakeholders prefer not to read a long report, but to see the important information set out succinctly. A single A4 sheet was all I was allowed to use to communicate progress each week, when I was leading my most rewarding 2 year project. The progress report looked a bit like this.

Planned for Previous Week • Tasks • Cost • Dates	Achieved in Previous Week • Tasks • Cost • Dates
Variances from Plan Recommended Actions	Planned for Next Week (to be approved)

Remember the communications plan you built earlier to remind you who to send it to and *how* you should communicate.

It may be a formal meeting, which might be weekly or monthly, depending on your stakeholders' requirement as laid down in the communications plan. You would let them know of any under spend, over spend, early completion of tasks or delays. As the project manager it is then up to you to recommend a way forward, request any additional help (funds or deadline changes) and put forward a rational argument for your recommendations.

REPORTING TO THE WORKERS

When you report to the workers it may, similarly, be informal or formal. Again this depends on the size of project and whether or not you are working with /for someone else.

Assuming you are doing the refurbishment of a modest residential property, using individual trades and looking after the ordering of the main materials such as paint, bathroom suites, appliances, kitchen units, I would suggest an informal meeting. Just don't call it "a meeting". Arrange to drop by the property once a week with the specific purpose of catching up on how things are going.

Turn up when you say you will. Make the meeting more like a chat over a short break. Bring with you details of any other dependent trades not able to keep to previously agreed dates, delivery dates for materials (and information about whether or not you are going to be there to check it in) and crucially your availability over the next week. Explain if there is any issue with stakeholders, such as funding or deadlines. On a small residential refurbishment project, keep the workers informed about the welfare side of things, such as when you are replenishing the biscuits and coffee. What is little matter to you may be important to Mr Fixit. Keep everyone in the picture.

If you are working on a large project, your workers may be a firm of builders. You will need to get the same sort of information (leaving aside the issue of biscuits) to the main contractor. This will be in the form agreed in the communications plan. Whether it is an informal meeting or something more formal, I recommend arranging for the meeting to be held on site. Bear in mind you could be meeting with several interested parties (site manager, architect, electrical contractor) in one meeting. Take minutes and ensure everyone involved has a copy and agrees them afterwards.

WORKERS REPORTING TO YOU

Although I have broken this down into specific elements, the workers generally report to you in the same meetings (get-togethers) as when you report to them, as I've outlined above. In the next step in the monitoring stage (Actuals) we can look a little more closely at the sort of things they are reporting to you and what to look out for. These may be details which the trades themselves do not consider important to you.

STAKEHOLDERS REPORTING TO YOU

Stakeholders generally report to you at the same time as you report to them. There is one big difference. Money.

Remember some types of loan are unregulated, as is the money you have set aside personally to support the project. This is not the place to go into the detail of establishing water tight contracts with JV partners, banks or crowd funders. It is possible that they may be obliged to call in funds they are lending you earlier than you expect. This is just about the worst event I'd expect a stakeholder to have to report to you. It is most likely to reach you in the form of a formal letter.

REPORT TO YOURSELF AS A STAKEHOLDER

For one moment consider reporting to yourself. I said something may seem odd. You have a budget (unless you skipped the planning chapter) and hopefully you have money in an account specifically for this project. That biscuit tin never earns interest. While monitoring your project you will have ascertained how much you have spent and how much you need to complete the project on time to your standards. Check your project account balance. I'd recommend, every week. You never know when you may need that contingency fund.

So much for reporting. Let's look at what *evidence* you can actually gather while you are monitoring.

ACTUALS

Gather data and make notes. Your day book comes in handy at this point. Date everything. Here we are going to look at actual data you can gather from a progress meeting, be it informal or formal.

You may not have been told everything. Always make notes and keep them in an *orderly* fashion for future reference. You may need these notes in five years' time when you are starting on a similar project. Keeping your notes will make future projects far easier to plan and estimate.

USE YOUR EYES FIRST

A lot can be discovered by simply using your eyes before you even start to ask questions of the people working on the ground, especially if you meet on site. Take a look around.

- Look at all the invoices for materials and labour so you know what you have spent.
- On site, look at what has happened. See if it appears to be in order or in chaos. Make your own judgement about what work has and has not been done. Observe which tasks have been completed. Completed according to a plumber may not be completed to you.
- On site, look and see what materials have and have not been delivered.
- On site, notice what rubbish is being accumulated and think about health and safety.
- On site, check the welfare facilities are all OK. Running out of toilet rolls can spell disaster, or at least discontent.
- On site, look at the standard of the finish in terms of colour, texture, fittings used.

- Where there is more than one trade working on site at the same time, look at body language and see if there is any friction or practical contention for space.

USE YOUR EARS

Whether on site, on the telephone, via Skype or at a mutually convenient place chosen for you to meet with each person working on the project, there are a few key questions you need to ask. Then use your ears. Listen carefully and keep notes. The key questions are as follows:

- What have you made a start on this week?
- What proportion of the task has been done? E.g. is it half way through or about 25%?
- How many days has each task been worked on?
- How many more days do you need to finish each task?
- Which tasks have you finished this week? It often helps to use a copy of the job specification and tick off what has been done.

Beware, the way someone answers your questions may not correspond directly, so just take notes and analyse later.

The key question to *never* ask is? "How is it going?" Ask that and you know the answer, don't you? "It's fine". That answer tells you absolutely nothing. You need to gather actual facts.

USE YOUR HANDS

Yes, you can run your hands over the paint finish if you want, but I am more concerned with collecting up evidence.

Pick up all evidence to take back and analyse when you have time away from the refurbishment site. What am I talking about? Well, you will need to collect up the following:

- Invoices that you will need to pay. These are from contractors who have completed work or with whom you have agreed stage payments. Invoices from suppliers may have been sent to you directly, but make sure you keep them all together
- Delivery notes for materials delivered directly to site
- Time sheets (if you are using them) from contractors / workers / trades persons
- Odd notes from contractors. People sometimes jot down on a piece of paper what they intend to let you know, then forget when it comes to having a chat / progress meeting. I suggest to my contractors that it might be easier to use sticky notes, in situ, than to remember things for a week. You may also get odd notes in email form. Keep all the evidence you can together. It really helps as the project progresses

So, I hope you feel a bit happier about gathering actual data, keeping notes and evidence to help you manage your project. If you monitor actual progress, using the guidelines I've just outlined, you can put your notes aside, even take a day off if you so choose, and work on them later. At least you have the wherewithal to know where your project is and how it is going.

I have suggested making use of all your key senses. No more does this hold true than in identifying problems.

HAVE A NOSE FOR PROBLEMS

If a project throws up absolutely no challenges and there are no problems or stumbling blocks, only a couple of alternative explanations spring to mind. Either you are superman/ superwoman project manager or you are kidding yourself about the project. I doubt you are superman / woman. I may be wrong, but if I am, why are you reading this guide?

TOO SMALL TO CALL IT A PROJECT?

Was it so small a task it could hardly be called a project? Sadly I've been assigned to very small projects in the public sector, where a heavily formalised project management method was used to manage a one week "project" involving only a handful of people and only costing the salaries. Salaries are sunk costs anyway, so I ponder on what was true benefit?

Pragmatism rules in my world, which is why much of my approach to project work calls upon the principles and not the straight jacket of formal methods. If managing the project takes up more time (and hence cost) than the work on the ground, then it becomes a problem in itself. My PUMA process is a pragmatic framework that leaves a lot of the over formalisation of big business aside and focusses on the essentials that help entrepreneurial investor landlords like you.

KIDDING YOURSELF?

More often we can be tempted to kid ourselves that there is not really an issue and the project will work out fine in the end. Promise me you will resist said temptation. Please. For your own sake. You have come this far. You have undertaken progress reporting meetings. You have collected up all the evidence on progress you can, both on site and off site. You have almost all you need to identify real (not imagined) problems. Delve deep and make notes.

You know how to gather data and make notes, using your eyes, hands and voice as well as your ears. Ask yourself if something needs your intervention. If someone on your workforce team just "mentioned" an issue in passing, delve into it more thoroughly. Ask more open questions, as well as those which can have a "yes" or "no" answer. It may turn out not to be an issue. Listen. Observe reactions. Watch for behaviour patterns. If someone fails to turn up to meet you a few times, or is frequently late, make a note to yourself and look for more information before taking action. Don't kid yourself everything is just fine; it may not be. If someone is showing signs of stress, ask more questions; the reasons why might be something that can be overcome quite quickly with or without your help.

HEALTH & SAFETY PROBLEMS

Problems can emerge in respect of health and safety aspects of the project. Never overlook health and safety. Look for anyone cutting corners. Make sure that any accidents or near misses have been reported promptly. Take pictures if possible; you are gathering evidence. Health and safety issues can knock your project off track. If one person goes down with some bug and you don't have effective control measures in place (e.g. antibacterial hand wash and hot water) you may see the whole team knocked out of action for some time.

AN INCIDENT BOOK

Always make notes. Ensure you keep notes about each and every incident, be it an accident or a near miss. Include dates, times, people involved, equipment or facilities in place or not up to scratch. Record every detail, including pictures of any physical or practical issues, such as damaged toilets, trip hazards, so that they can be dealt with in a timely fashion. You may choose to keep incidents and accidents in a separate "incident book", rather than in the project manager's day book. Review the incident book each time you visit your project site.

ALL SHAPES & SIZES

Challenges and problems come in all shapes and sizes, from biscuits and the weather to Building Control. Some need your intervention. Others do not. Being aware of any problems, ideally before they develop into a crisis, is more than half the battle. The other half is taking appropriate action.

ESTIMATES TO GO

There is just one more thing to ask as you monitor project progress, but it is key.

Ask each member of the team (contractors/ workers/ trades) *when* they expect to have the job done. How much longer do they believe we have to go before the task is complete? This may not be the same as the date you work out later.

Once when I was working for someone whom I looked up to in the business world, I realised the importance of this question. He was my boss. I was the project manager. Following one of my team's traumatic car accident, my boss was helping her avoid the unnecessary stress of our routine monitoring process.

So, it was my boss I had to ask the key question of. I can be impatient and nice chit chat has no place in my professional work, especially during projects with a tight deadline. He fell back in his chair laughing, saying something along the lines of "spoken like a true project manager". Flattered? Sure I was. As he was also responsible for my annual performance appraisals I felt good about that outbreak of laughter.

It is vitally important to ask the question as to what specific date the person responsible for the task expects to complete it.

STRAIGHT LINE OR ZIGZAG

Having been a keen yachtswoman in my youth and taken part in a number of races, I am always on the lookout for things not going quite as planned. There may be a straight line from the start point to the destination on my chart, but it only takes one squall or a slight change in wind direction to miss the destination altogether. It only takes one member of the crew (project team) to lack concentration, however briefly, to make the difference between first and second place.

Me keeping an eye on how the wind (project progress) is shifting.

With your own and other people's financial position at stake, you must monitor your project. Keep an eye on how the project is straying from the plan. You may have to take a turn here or there and not follow the straight line you planned. Managing how far you go off that straight line is up to you, but it has to be your conscious choice.

Now, armed with a wealth of data, what do you imagine might happen if you simply file your notes and forget about them? Yes, you can take a day off now and again, but don't leave too much time between collecting your evidence, along with taking notes and *doing* something with that evidence. What do you imagine might happen if I sailed some five degrees off my course when heading for Calais and did nothing about it for six hours or so? I might end up in Dunkirk (or worse).

Now is the time to ANALYSE the data so that you are able to make those decisions which will keep your project on track.

Key points to remember
• Simple is not necessarily easy • A Project Manager's Day Book for keeping notes • Spot challenges before they become a crisis • Use all your senses, sight, hearing, speech, touch, smell • Collect evidence, invoices, timesheets, delivery notes • Ask what date the person responsible for each task expects to complete it • Incident / Accident Book • Avoid headaches - keep an eye on the detail

CHAPTER 10 ANALYSE

I am an AVID analyser. In some areas of life this could be called "being a control freak". In project management, be it property refurbishment or any other project, the ability to analyse the data you gather is crucial if you intend to complete the project successfully. I enjoy analysing (the fourth stage in our PUMA process) how things are really going and not just relying on what I may be told.

- **A**ctuals compared to Plan
- **V**ariances
- **I**ndicators
- **D**ecisions

Love your software and enjoy developing a completely clear picture of exactly what point your project has reached. Spreadsheets suffice for some small to medium sized property refurbishment projects. For those larger projects you'll need to fall in love with specific project management software.

Become an avid analyser. Understand the implications of the data you have gathered in order to make informed decisions.

COMPARE ACTUAL DATA TO THE PLAN

We need to regularly compare the data we have gathered during our monitoring, against our current plan. I find weekly is about the right interval between each analysis, until I am nearing the end of a project on a tight deadline.

Find somewhere quiet which is outside the bustle and chatter of a progress meeting. Ideally find somewhere you can concentrate and refer to earlier documents, compare the evidence you have gathered against the dates, times and costs you documented in your work plan. Why would you need a quiet space? Well, this is where you will need to use all your reasoning and analytical skills and it is where you will have to make the big decisions.

If you don't do any comparison you may never know that the entire project is not going to finish on time, or that it may cost more than your budget. Imagine being close to the end of the project and running out of money (yours or perhaps your JV partner's). Imagine having to go back to the bank for extra funds shortly before they are expecting to be repaid.

We've all seen those properties which come onto the market part refurbished, where work has come to a halt. They may well represent an opportunity to property investors. However, I imagine you don't want it to be you who is the one having to sell up because you failed to do the analysis of what you have seen or been told during progress visits to the project site.

Actual dates and costs are reflected in the data you gather, be it by your own observation or from what various trades-people have told you, or given you on timesheets, when you asked. The plan tells you when you expected to do what and at what cost. Compare each aspect to see if they differ.

ONE TASK AT A TIME

Look at each task on the work plan, one at a time. Look at the cost so far and the cost you expected for that particular task. Look at the end date you have been given by the plumber, carpenter, supplier or whoever, along with your own opinion of when the task is likely to complete. On the work plan, note down the actual cost, based on invoices and time sheets, all of which will need to be paid on time. On the work plan also note down the revised end date. When you monitor the time it takes to do a particular task, make a note of how long it is actually taking. You can do this easily using some sort of software such as MsProject or you can include columns in your spreadsheet.

Let's consider an example. The principles are the same whether you use a spreadsheet or project management software. We'll look at just two tasks in what would be a much larger work plan.

Task	Est Days Work	Planned Start	Planned End	Planned Cost	Actual work	Actual Start	Actual/ revised End	Actual cost	Complete
Clear garden	5	01/02/18	08/02/18	£500	2	07/02/18	11/02/18		
Replace garden fence	2	09/02/18	10/02/18	£800					

The right-hand column is where we indicate whether or not the task is complete. Just because the actual / revised end date is filled in does not mean the task of clearing the garden is complete.

Let's assume, in this simple example, that you monitored what was going on at a site visit on Thursday 08/02 afternoon. Although this is a simplification and your real project may have hundreds of tasks and you will have more columns than shown here (e.g. dependencies and which resources are allocated to each task), we can still understand quite a lot from it.

When you visited the site you could see for yourself that the garden had not been cleared. The chap you hired to clear the garden started later than planned, yet he assures you that if he gets a move on it will only be two more days work and he can finish up by 11/02/18. As that is a Sunday, you may wish to go back and ask for clarification; he may not be able to finish until the end of day on Monday 12/02. Had he finished work on clearing the garden you would simply put the letter C in the right hand column to indicate to yourself that this is completed and there is no more work or cost associated with that particular task.

You can now see from this small degree of analysis that there is a clash. The fencing contractor you have booked in for 09/02 might potentially arrive while the garden is still being cleared.

So what now? Now you need to repeat logging what has happened and what looks more likely for every task in the work plan before focussing on the variances. Update the work plan to reflect progress both reported to you and observed by you.

VARIANCES

Variances are the differences between what was planned and what actually has happened. You can see if the cost is going to be greater than anticipated. You can see if one part of the work is running so late that it may hold up tasks that are dependent on it. You can see when your overall project is going to be finished. It might be going to finish earlier or later than planned.

If you are formally reporting to a project board or to a JV (joint venture) partner, it is most likely that you will need to look at three key elements:

- Cost variances
- Date variances
- Time effort, that is the number of days the task takes, variances

For a small to medium sized residential property refurbishment, I focus on costs and dates of when different jobs are started or completed, using the people you have chosen to work with. I concern myself less with how many days the contractor put in because I tend to negotiate a fixed price.

The principles are exactly the same. A spreadsheet can subtract one amount of money from another, one date from another or a number of days from another, using an easy formula. Project management software generally does this automatically without the need for you to even input a formula.

DON'T IGNORE CASH FLOWS

Muddling along is going to cost you more, so make sure you sit down with a cup of tea/ coffee or whatever and have a word with yourself. Ask "have I got sufficient money to do what I'm trying to do?" If not, you have decisions to make. We can look at decision making in more detail later. I think you would agree it is more professional to monitor how much you have spent as you go along rather than have a shock later?

Cost overrun can kill. Less dramatically it can lead to an unwelcomely large overdraft, bad relationship with partners, missing out on a tenant or buyer you had lined up or embarrassment. You will not get it right first time, but you have to start somewhere. By planning well in the first place and analysing what you see and hear going on within the project you will live to fight another day and run another even more successful project. I want to know what I have spent and what I am going to have to shell out in the future. Perhaps most importantly, if I am relying on my bank for funds, I want to know how much I am going to need and when.

Let's look at the variances in the example we have just considered. I'll substitute a few columns so that this is easier to see. I have altered a few entries so that we can understand the concept of variances more readily. In practice you need to keep all the columns and then select which columns you wish to see during your analysis and for when you prepare a progress report. You can hide or reveal columns with project management software and similarly with most spreadsheets.

Task	Est Day	Planned Start	Planned End	Planned Cost	Actual work	Actual Cost so far	Actual/ revised End	Cost Var	End Var
Clear garden	5	01/02/18	08/02/18	£500	2	£200	10/02/18	£300 under	2 days late
Replace garden fence	2	09/02/18	10/02/18	£800					

Let's say that the progress meeting was held late on 08/02. All evidence is as at that date. So, as at 08/02 we have the chap clearing the garden telling you that although he should have finished and has only put in two days, he can still complete the job in the next two days. By taking one date (08/02 the planned end date) from another (the actual or revised end date of 10/02) you can see that this part of your project is going to be two days late. By taking the actual cost from the planned cost (your budget) we see that so far this task has cost £300 less than we had expected at this time. Yes, there are other things to consider. Working out variances is a purely mechanistic job you need to do. It lends itself perfectly to software. Software would, generally speaking, use + and – signs and not "under", "over", "late" or "early", but you can set up a formula to make your work plan look and feel more user friendly.

VARIANCE (A DIFFERENCE) IN EFFORT

What is useful for your future projects is the variance in effort, or amount of work the person needs to put in. The gardener gave you a figure of £500 for five days' work. As three days have elapsed and he has only put in two days' work / effort and there are only two calendar days to go before he says he will be finished, you might reasonably say that this job will end up taking four days of work. If this was a man-day price (£100 per man day) then you should only be charged £400. Watch the invoice next time you monitor progress on this. So for any future project where a similar job is needed, you'll have a better idea of how long to plan for. I know, seldom are two jobs exactly the same. However a bathroom refit or small kitchen refit do tend to come out much the same in terms of the work required, each time around. It is more likely that any difference in cost estimate from one similar project to another is in the specific style and workmanship.

You don't want to be bogged down with our going through every element of even this simple example together, I am sure, but I trust you see the pattern. Whatever you planned in terms of time and money can be analysed to find the specific variances. It will then be over to you to decide what to do about it, but more of that later.

COMPARE QUALITY

The one thing we have not compared, so far, against what we planned is the quality of the job being done. Being partly subjective, this important element relies on your having set out the scope of the project during the planning stage. You will have done your best to express the standard / quality you want, unambiguously in the first place and on the strength of the specification of the work you prepared when unleashing the work force. Quality cannot really be measured in numbers, but you still need to watch out for quality differences as you monitor progress and the project progresses.

Check delivery notes and invoices against what you asked for. One obvious variance is the make or style of fittings; if you asked for a specific brand of paint and notice DIY store invoices or own brand cans around the site, I'd suspect there is a variation between what you specified and what you are getting. If you specified a particular make of taps and ended up with contract taps, someone is cutting corners, or not paying attention to what you really asked for. If you specified that the second fix electrical work should include making good, make sure you check that the plaster *has or has not* been made good around new switches and sockets.

INDICATORS

Once you have gathered all your data, have sat down and entered your new end dates, actual costs and actual work effort into whatever software you are using, you should have a good idea about how far your project is departing from your original plan. This is in terms of number of days or completion dates difference (time), quality, and the variance between your budget and what you now project the overall cost to be.

Now you need to analyse what you have seen or sensed in conjunction with your figures. Intuition does have a part to play at this stage, although some might argue I really mean experience and insightfulness. Whatever we call it, we need to look out for various non-arithmetic indicators.

Project management software can flag up where conflicts, overlaps between jobs that cannot realistically be done at the same time, and gaps where you could be getting something done but nothing is likely to happen. Yes, you can use your spreadsheet skills to see where conflict, overlaps or gaps occur in the project. In a simple cosmetic or light property refurbishment, a spreadsheet works just fine. For something more extensive, perhaps a house conversion to flats, I would strongly recommend investing in software.

CONFLICT EXAMPLE

In our earlier example we had two tasks, the first to clear a garden and another to erect fencing around the garden. The probability, unless you do most of the work yourself, is that fencing contractors will have been booked in for your planned start date for installing the fencing. Looking at the new anticipated end date for the garden clearance and the start date for the fencing, you can see that that fencing contractors are going to turn up while someone is thrashing about clearing the garden. Will they get in one another's way? Your analysis has shown you that there is an overlap between these tasks.

Your chap doing the garden clearance is running late. His anticipated finish date is later than you planned for. Time for a spot of analysis. Why is he running late? Was the weather too bad to start on time? Was he unwell for part of the time? If you have used the same chap previously, does he often start late and overrun? What about the quality of the work? If you asked for all weeds and plants to be removed, have they just had their heads cut off, leaving the roots to come back? Do the fencing contractors know him and if so, how well might they work together? If you ask the fencing contractors to postpone their work, is it practical and will it cost you more to change at this stage? Crucially, look ahead through the project work plan and ask yourself what impact does it have on anyone else booked in, not to mention the overall end date?

BEHAVIOUR PATTERNS

Look for patterns in the data and of behaviour. Generally, if someone is frequently taking longer to complete a task than you planned (or you consider reasonable), you should see a pattern emerging. One thing I have fallen foul of is the fitter who prefers to work while no-one else is on site and then fails to complete the work on time. Learn from my mistakes. In spite of your regular monitoring you may not be able to see the real problem at first. If this happens more than once or twice, it is an indication of things to come and I would have doubts about not only the timing but the quality. Having had a couple of bad experiences, I can say that lone working is sometimes an indication that the person has accepted the job for the money but lacks the experience to do it well, regardless of references and insurances. These days I steer clear of those who want to work out of my sight *all* of the time.

Someone working on your project might be more irritable or tired than usual. Explore whether this is an indicator of stress, worry or ill health. Try to understand why, what impact it may be having on that person as well as on your project. With people you don't know well, there is a limit to what you can ask. Be sensitive, use your own experience of people and analyse what could be the problem but don't be presumptuous.

BALANCED ANALYSIS

Be balanced in your analysis. Analysis is about comparing data, asking more questions, spotting patterns, sensing where things are about to go wrong and assessing the impact on your project overall. But, don't overdo it. If the project is only three or four months long, then spending a whole day each week analysing the data might be a bit too much. On a small project you may well be mentally doing the analysis at the same time as monitoring progress. I have separated these processes out so that you can see how to systematically go about keeping on top of any sized property refurbishment project.

Beware the paralysis of analysis.

You, and only you (as you are managing the refurbishment) are going to have to make decisions. Imagine burying your head in the sand and making no decisions at all, in spite of seeing a few tasks not going according to plan. No decisions? No action? Worse still are you going to abdicate and let someone else take over the responsibility for making decisions? What is the most likely outcome then? May I suggest that your project will take longer to complete, will go over budget and will not be what you wanted!

DECISIONS

It's up to you to make the decisions. That is, unless you report to a project board which tends to apply to a larger project. You still need to decide what you believe to be the best course of action and recommend it, allowing them to believe they made the decisions. Whether the board takes up your recommendations or not is a far more involved matter.

With the best will in the world it is not unusual for something to go wrong and differ from your plan on most refurbishment projects. Something will go wrong. Why? Simply because property and project management are both "people businesses" and people are complex, with many things going on in each life independently of one another.

You will need to consider *all* the options (possible courses of action) and the likely impact in terms of time, money and quality of each on other parts of the project. By being decisive, communicating your decisions right away (refer to your communications plan) and keeping the overall aims and critical success factors of your project in mind (refer to the scope you wrote up), you maximise the probability of project success.

To help you consider all the options I find it helps to ask these questions:

- Can someone else pick up work that is lagging behind?
- Can you use alternative suppliers if materials cannot be delivered on time?

- Can some other tasks be started earlier / later without compromising what comes further on?
- Can more people be put onto a task at the same time?
- Can some tasks be done in a different sequence?
- Does someone need to have time off the project?
- Will extra people enable the project to complete on time?
- Will extra money solve the problem? How much? When?
- Will we achieve the requisite standard if we use different materials?

*How*ever you answer these questions and *what*ever you answer, keep asking yourself "what are we going to do?" You are the person to answer that. That is your job. Keep looking for alternatives before the situation becomes a major issue that might compromise the success of your project.

What are we going to do? The answer is up to you!

CONSIDERING ALTERNATIVES

You can decide to get some more money from somewhere or revise the scope of your project to perhaps use less expensive materials and fittings. Alternatively you could use a less expensive contractor, but there must have been a reason to use the one you have in the first place. In making a decision you will have to mentally juggle *all* the forces on your project, both internal and external to it. There are so many factors involved that your decision may turn out not to be the best in hindsight. Hindsight is a wonderful thing, but each week decisions you must make. I'm sure you already have a mental list of the sort of things to weigh up in coming to a decision, but perhaps a list of the main things I consider may help.

- Tasks not started on time
- Tasks taking longer than expected
- Materials not being delivered, or delivered late
- Suppliers going out of business
- Materials being invoiced at the wrong price
- The effect of weather on the work
- Unexpected new tasks becoming necessary
- Running out of money
- Interest rate rises
- Larger expenses on the horizon than planned
- Lenders needing their money back early
- Estimates changing
- Welfare facilities not proving adequate
- Compliance issues or changes in legislation
- Health / stress
- Bereavement
- Skills not coming up to your standard

The above list is not exhaustive, but it may help you start thinking. Thinking alone is unlikely to be enough on anything other than the simplest of refurbishments. It helps, I believe, to have a process to help us reach the best decisions we can at any one time.

IMPACT ANALYSIS

An impact analysis is often used to consider alternative ways forward. Of course, if there is only one way forward there is no need; the decision is made for you. So, what is an impact analysis? It is the step by step approach to looking at alternative solutions and identifying what the likely impact is going to be of each alternative.

Let's look again at the simple problem of the garden clearance running late compared to what you had planned.

Solution	**Impact on Costs**	**Impact on Time**	**Impact on Quality**	**Impact on People**
Do nothing	None	None. Should stay on track	Less neat fencing	Friction with Fencing contractors
Stop garden clearance	May reduce costs if a man day rate was agreed. Wasted money if fixed price	None. Brings the project back on track	Garden not as clear as required May not be good enough for next task	Less than happy gardener unless he has another job to go to
Postpone fencing	Likely to increase costs	Fencing contractor availability may hinder the project	None likely	Fencing contractor may be less likely to want to work with you again
Split timing of garden clearance	None likely	Gardener's availability may hinder project, but not too likely	Probably a little less thorough	Minor
Replace gardener	Replacement gardener may cost more.	Delay almost inevitable.	Potential for a better job.	Unlikely to be able to use the original gardener again.

Let's not forget the fact that "do nothing" is always one potentially acceptable solution. That is only if you have analysed the likely impact on the main project factors of cost, time and quality, whilst taking into consideration the people working on the project and with whom you may wish to work in the future.

A word of caution might be appropriate here; if this is all you use you are *not* an expert. What I have described is a *simplified* impact analysis.

In a thorough impact analysis you would have columns for the probability of the impact occurring and not be using words to indicate how likely the impact is. Probabilities of LOW (unlikely), MEDIUM, HIGH (likely) would be attributed a numerical factor so that subjectivity is removed from the analysis. You'd also need to consult with more than one other person, e.g. to ascertain specific additional costs.

Armed with the simplified version, you should be feeling more comfortable, more decisive, and able to spot problems early and deal with them before they become a crisis.

USE SKILLS AND EXPERIENCE YOU ALREADY HAVE

You probably don't realise what skills you already have that are useful in your property refurbishments. Everything you have experienced is for a purpose. You are unique and always will be. Your style of project management may well follow the PUMA process I use, but your past experiences will colour *how* you manage and *what sort* of projects you manage.

Not only can you make good use of your own unique past, but your understanding can be enhanced by learning from other people's experiences and a few of my mistakes.

COWBOYS AND INDIANS

As a child I was taken to see "Cowboys and Indians" films on Friday afternoon. Whenever the Apache Indians (always Apaches in these old films) were seen by the wagon train scouts, lined up on horseback on the horizon, someone would gallop back and organise the wagons into a defensive circle. By analysing what they saw before an attack occurred, the leader/ hero was always able to set up his new position to give the settlers the best chance of reaching their destination safely.

It is up to you, as the property project manager, to see issues developing *before* they become a crisis and to make decisions. So, spot "Apaches" (challenges) on the Horizon (against your plan) before they attack (time, money or quality problems) your project. As most Apache Indians are certainly no threat in real life, so not all challenges or variances from plan are necessarily threats to your project.

Keep a look out for challenges looming on the horizon.

By keeping a good look out, facing challenges and addressing potential issues early on you can avoid seriously injurious problems. In that way you should minimise headaches and sleepless nights. Having spotted challenges and made decisions, what do you think you must do? You need to go back to the original plan, take a fresh look armed with the data you have gathered and analysed, then make changes based on your decisions. Check the revised plan for reasonableness. Report back to stakeholders and make sure those working on the project are kept in the picture and know of any change of work allocation, timescales and budgets. People need to know about changes to plan, why they are being made and what impact such changes will have on each one of them.

SMALL PERSISTENT FLAPS

In the context of his work as a meteorologist, Edward Lorenz came to reflect on an intriguing question. The question, which he presented in an academic paper in 1972 entitled "Predictability" was as follows "does the flap of a butterfly's wings in Brazil set off a Tornado in Texas?" His suggestion that *many small movements can cause a huge impact*, is relevant to managing a project. The butterfly moves his wings just a little, over and over again consistently: being *persistent and consistent*, is key to success in achieving bigger things. We just need persistent small steps, small flaps, small manageable tasks, small adjustments at any one time and you can get the property refurbishment job done, with a high degree of control.

Make small adjustments often.

In your property journey you can achieve whatever you want to achieve, even if you are a little nervous, by being open to learning from others and by being persistent and consistent.

It may only take a few minor scheduling or people changes to enable you to complete your project on time, within budget and to your own high standard. Aim for perfection but accept that perfection is seldom attainable.

It may only take half a dozen minor increases in cost or time to make the difference between completing on time, within budget, to the requisite standard whilst preserving your sanity, and overspending, overrunning or enduring sleepless nights. Costs often worry investors. If you complete within your contingency, you are still within budget; that is still a successfully managed project.

On the subject of money to fund property projects, Gill Fielding gave me three words of encouragement that repeatedly crop up in thinking about refurbishment projects in several different ways: *"yes you can".* You just have to make the decision to do it. Regardless of what barriers are put in your way, you can find property, you can fund it, you can refurbish it (one small task at a time) and you can achieve your wider goals.

Remember Lorenz's butterfly effect? If a butterfly can have such an impact with many small wing flaps, you can be successful by making many small adjustments to your project.

Key points to remember
• Compare what is actually happening (time, budget and quality standard) to your plan • Compare progress against your Critical Success Factors – remember you set them out in the scope document? • Use the unique skills you already have • Look for patterns of behaviour • Beware the paralysis of analysis - balanced • Make small adjustments often – a butterfly flapping? • Spot problems on the horizon before they become a threat to your project • Ask yourself, what are we going to do about it? • Be persistent and consistent

CHAPTER 11 RINSE AND REPEAT

SEVERAL CYCLES

Following your analysis, which is the last of the four stages of the PUMA process, you'll need to simply rinse and repeat. Just go round the four stages again until you reached the planned end. Project management is a cyclical process.

You may need several rinses. Sometimes, in your considered opinion during the analysis, there will be no need to drastically alter the plan at all. At other times, through experience of what is happening on the ground as your project progresses, you will need to go back and rework the plan, perhaps just a couple of times. How many times you go round the cycle is up to you. You are the person responsible for making the decisions. This is what the puma learns and how she constantly monitors the situation, analyses her options, watches how the wind shifts, then adjusts her hunting plan to get dinner.

BACK UP AND COMMUNICATE

Before making any changes to your plan, I'd suggest you keep the original plan, take a copy and then make changes. This is in order that you have the wherewithal to return to the original if necessary; things can go wrong.

When you modify your plan you should change whatever needs changing and leave what is working as it is. You can change (yes, I mean in your documented plan) any tasks, resources, estimates, allowances for contingency or dependencies.

Remember to make sure all the people involved in the project are kept in the picture by issuing the current version of the work plan and any associated documents in a timely fashion.

Learning from experience on the actual project as it unfolds (few projects are exactly the same) and making adjustments is what I mean by rinsing. Do this then repeat each of the stages, **P**lan, **U**nleash, **M**onitor, **A**nalyse.

The following diagram will help fix the general process in your mind. You can use it as a reference guide for future projects.

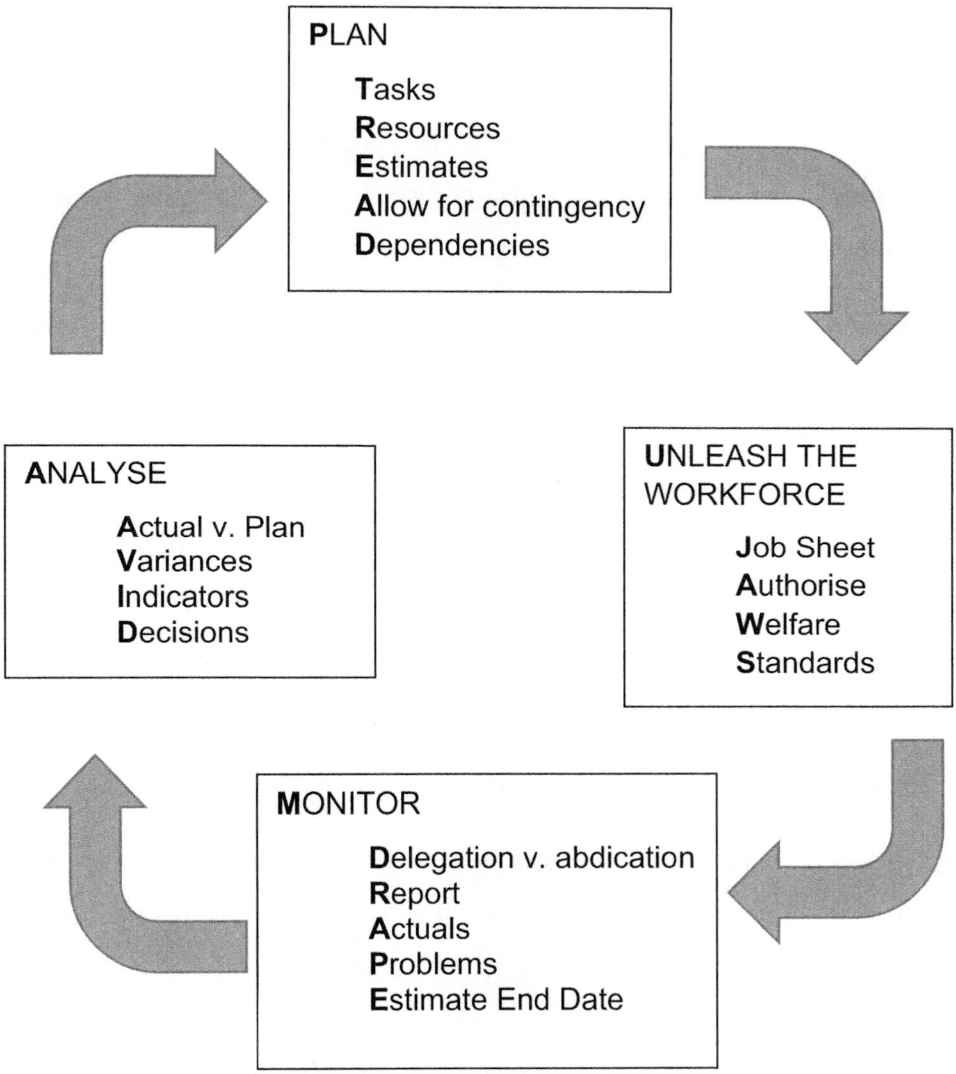
PLAN
Tasks
Resources
Estimates
Allow for contingency
Dependencies
UNLEASH THE WORKFORCE
Job Sheet
Authorise
Welfare
Standards
MONITOR
Delegation v. abdication
Report
Actuals
Problems
Estimate End Date
ANALYSE
Actual v. Plan
Variances
Indicators
Decisions

COMING TO A CONCLUSION

Like a washing machine which repeats its cycle, including several rinses, there comes a time when the project cycle comes to its conclusion. The drum stops going round. It is time to admire the clean laundry / finished property.

There comes a time when all that data you have gathered needs to be put to one further good use. Use the corrected estimates for a task and the actual costs of materials and labour to inform the planning stage of your next project. There is no more need to rinse and repeat the process within the project once the property has been sold or let. You have made it. You should reward yourself and reflect on your success in the same way the puma enjoys her lunch.

POST REFURBISHMENT REVIEW

As soon as the refurbishment has been completed take another look at your final conclusions from the evidence you have. In many industries and certainly during most of my own time as an employee, we would call it the Post Implementation Review. In the property arena it can be called something different. In our situation let's call this a Post Refurbishment Review. This may be over a well-earned cup of coffee (or something stronger, as you wish), a meal with your partner or a formal meeting involving the whole team. It all depends on the size of the project, the nature of the project and the people involved in it along the way.

However you organise the review, please don't forget to do it. You need to reflect on what you have learned during the project. Once you have completed the final analysis against time, budget and quality, return to the scope you set in the first place. Check each "critical success factor" and make sure you have achieved what you set out to. Admire your property. Ask a few key questions, including:

- What went well?
- What went wrong or less well?
- Would you do anything differently next time?
- Are you in love with the property?
- Will someone such as the person or people you originally thought about, fall in love with it?
- Are the trades you hired happy to work with you again?

Key points to remember
• Back up the original plan so that you can go back to it if you need to • Project management is a cyclical process • Learn from experience on the actual project and make adjustments as required • Repeat the planning stage only if it is necessary • Communicate any changes of plan to everyone before repeating the four stage process • Review how the project went once it reaches its conclusion – be honest

CHAPTER 12 TIME TO SMELL THE ROSES

Let's step back and think about the puma, whom I admire so much. Each hunt is carefully planned. She watches and monitors her prey, remains aware of the terrain and attends to her own stamina, analysing the situation and making small adjustments and adapting her hunt to achieve her goal. Then she sits back, guards her dinner, feeds her cubs, eats her fill and finally relaxes. When your project ends successfully, why shouldn't you copy the example of the puma and relax?

TO STRESS OR NOT TO STRESS

When someone said to me at a property networking meeting that project management is one of the most stressful aspects of property investing, I was curious. I'm not so sure it has to be. As we know, zero stress equals inertia, so we all need some positive energising stress.

You could of course hire a project manager if you decide not to manage your own refurbishment projects. It pays, however, to know the fundamental process which I have shared with you in the four stage project process I use. You also need to understand what has to be done and why, not necessarily how. You need to know that a qualified electrician is required to fit a new consumer unit and comply with regulations, but you do not necessarily need to know *how* to do it yourself.

Similarly, you don't need to do your own book keeping and tax returns. A good tax accountant can save you a whole heap of money, so let the expert do what he / she is good at and take time to relax once you have successfully completed the project.

Stick with what you are good at; there is no need to stress over what you are less good at. As Charles Handy would say, "stick with the knitting".

There will be times when you will feel the need to de-stress. There are other times when managing your refurbishment can be great fun. As your project comes to a successful conclusion you have earned some YOU time. You have earned time to be with family and friends and relax.

The wonderful lady who taught me most of what I know about property investing and doing up distressed property gave me this very important piece of advice:

Take time to smell the roses – a pearl from Gill Fielding

LEARNING FROM THOSE WHO WENT BEFORE YOU

Learning from those who have been through the early days of property investing and doing up property is the best way to move your property career forward, with less stress and more speedily than if you go it alone. It can save you time, money and sleepless nights. That is not to denigrate the value of formal training; it has an equally important place in your overall development.

Learning from those who have already made mistakes and "got the T shirt" will leave you with more time to smell the roses or do whatever takes your fancy, and spend time with who you want when you want. After a brisk sail, to get cleaned up and stretch out on the boom, out of everyone else's way, at the end of the day in some sunny port is my idea of relaxation.

Learn to chill out. This sentiment is reflected by Scott Alexander in his uniquely humorous, yet inspiring, book "Rhinoceros Success ".

Take off for one week and go lie in a mud hole. Do nothing but relax. Scott Alexander.

Then plan your next project?

Key points to remember
• Use positive energising stress • Learn to relax • Take time to smell the roses • Go lie in a mud hole and chill out when the project is successfully complete

CHAPTER 13 THAT MYSTICAL NUMBER THREE

Is the number three a magic number for property success? Remember "yes, you can". Just for fun here are a few thoughts, for you to think about as you rest and relax.

CHAOS IN MATHEMATICS

Mathematicians might suggest the entire universe is controlled (or at least explained) by numbers. I had doubted this, being something of a dunce at maths during my school years. Now you've probably heard this before;

The person you become is a reflection of what you read and the people who you mix with.

When a very good friend showed me a book on chaos theory and I saw in the fly that it was about mathematics I hesitated, well froze if I am honest with you. Anyone tackling some sort of property refurbishment will see times when things do look like chaos without much resemblance to maths. This theory suggests that there are patterns that will emerge. Form your own opinion on this, but let's reflect on that number three which has emerged from property refurbishments.

THE THREE AGES OF LIFE

When I first heard of the University of the 3rd Age (U3A) I didn't realise what it was. Google it if you are curious. Think about life. Not in too much depth. We all come into the world as a child, live as a child and then move on to adulthood. The first age of life is childhood. The second is adulthood, when some might start investing. The third age is older (not old, please) when many are retired and at last, enjoying the fruits of their labours/ investments and refurbishments. Not only does the number three control our basic life cycle, but it has quite an influence on property investment too.

THE PATTERN OF DAILY LIFE

It may seem obvious, but your daily life tends to be controlled by the number three. There are 24 hours in each day, no matter who you are. Most of us sleep for around one third of the time, work one third of the time and have one third – just eight hours – free to do what we want.

It is in those last eight hours of "free" time when you can choose to invest in property. So, why waste a single one of them. By using the PUMA framework to organise and run your property refurbishment project, you are most likely to be making the best use of every hour.

THREE TRADES IN ONE PLACE AT THE SAME TIME

While there is no hard and fast rule, three different trades working on a small residential property refurbishment at the same time is about the most I can handle. Build that into your work plan. Have you noticed that many small to medium sized builders (I'm thinking of the size of the business, not the individual) turn up with just three people (he who is in charge, he who does most of the skilled work and the apprentice who does the running about and clearing up). I apologise to all builders if that is too much of a generalisation. It is my observation. Property is a people business and that includes those people undertaking work on your property. As the project manager, it is up to you to resolve any conflict of interest. Consider the physical size of the space being worked upon. Have you ever seen (or heard) five grown men trying to work on a two metre by three metre kitchen replacement? Chaos.

When you have more than one property refurbishment project in the same area at the same time, it significantly reduces the risks of people falling over one another or holding one another up, to offset the start dates. For example, plumbing starts in property A only once the first stage wiring is complete and the electrician moves on to property B, thus avoiding perhaps the plumber needing power and having none.

A GENERAL BUILDER'S THREE

At a property networking meeting, a well-respected builder/ property developer / refurbishment coach stated that there are only three steps to a property refurbishment project. I paraphrase.

1) Rip out all the old
2) First fix
3) Install the new

Fundamentally I can't argue with that. That sounds like a builder's perspective, but perhaps there is more to it. What do you think, now you have read this far?

A DEVELOPER'S THREE

I tend to listen to other people. It's not a bad idea. This rough guide to determining how much to pay for a parcel of land was quite a revelation when I first heard it. If you are intending to acquire a plot of land, build a new property (or several) and sell it on, I've heard that number three again. It has been suggested that the overall project's cost (at its simplest) can be allocated into three very roughly equal parts.

1) One third of the project money to be paid for the land
2) Another third (very roughly) to be allocated to the development
3) The rest is your profit

This helps determine a fair price to pay for the land. How? Once again, you need to keep the end in mind from the outset.

Research what you could sell the finished property or properties for before you buy the land and embark on a development project. Work out the development cost, including the necessary permissions (planning permission, building regulations and health and safety) along with legal work. You now know something very important. You know a fair price for the land and whether the project is viable or not. If the finished property can't be sold for approximately three times the development costs it is not the perfect project. Few projects are the *perfect* fit, but this is a valuable rule of thumb.

EXAMPLE DEVELOPER'S THREE

As a simple example, imagine a plot of land comes up for sale. After talking to estate agents, planners and building controls as well as looking at recent sold prices in that area, you come up with a figure for the possible sale price (SP) of, say, £450K. Suppose your development estimate is £150K, then you would not see the purchase price (PP) of the land being more than £150K, would you? So, if we rely on the number three to see if this is the right project for us, we just add the three parts: PP + Development + Profit = SP. In this simple example £150K + £150K +£150K = £450K looks like an OK project. Of course things are seldom so perfect and that is where your judgement and attitude to risk come in.

A PROJECT MANAGER'S THREE

As the person managing your project, be it a single refurbishment or your whole property business, you need to be on hand to tackle three key tasks:

1) To answer a myriad of questions
2) To make decisions
3) To keep everyone involved in the picture and provided with the things they need, when they need them, to get the job done.

A GRAZIER'S (FARMER OF LIVESTOCK) THREE

One of the UKs most successful property millionaires, Kevin Green (previously a farmer, who retains a love of his cows) bases much of his property business model on the number three. Since he holds more properties in the UK than any other investor I know, I consider it more than worthwhile to listen to his simple rule which I have duly followed. Put simply, it goes like this.

Invest in three properties, refurbish them, hold two as rentals and sell one on.

The one he sells at a profit (owing to Kevin's purchasing strategy which you can read more about in his book "The Rich Rules ") provides funds to repay debt (loans) on his portfolio. The two he holds as rentals then show an increased cash flow, because they are costing less in interest on loans. Using this three, two, one rule provides ever-increasing cash flow and lower gearing. Any loans taken out when the property was purchased are paid off within ten years. Alternatively you could use those funds as a deposit on the next property. Not a bad model, eh? It is a model I have used since I first started investing in residential property to refurbish and sell, or to refurbish and rent out.

AN INVESTOR'S THREE

Many who invest in property also invest in other arenas. I know, you may be saying there are many forms of property investment besides refurbishing residential property. True. Several high net worth individuals I have come across recommend not keeping all your eggs in one basket, but spreading investment across the following:

1) Property
2) Gold
3) Fine art – if you read Kevin Green's book you will be substituting fine art with gem stones.

Are you enjoying that cup of coffee? This chapter is meant to be fun. Smile please.

A COMBI-BOILER'S THREE (A WHIMSICAL EXAMPLE)

Many an investor landlord who undertakes a property refurbishment finds that small well-presented properties appeal to younger tenants. When dealing with a combi boiler (number one) in residential property (number two) rented out to someone with little life experience (number three), there are three things that almost always crop up.

- Over pressurising the boiler. Who knows why? I don't. Give them time and guidance and they learn, or as someone once told me "love 'em and they'll grow".
- Good Heating Engineers are like rocking horse droppings, hard to find and difficult to keep for any length of time before someone kicks up a stink.
- If the combi boiler seems to think it is a living organism, it can be mischievous, play tricks on you and mal function just for fun. This behaviour is most frequently observed when new tenants are just getting settled in.

Three engineer call outs and a direct three-word instruction to tenants to "leave it alone" usually solves the problem.

If you have been an investor landlord for a while I imagine this will ring a few bells. If the idea is new to you, just remember this anecdote when you get a call about your combi-boiler going wrong in the middle of the night.

Key points to remember
• The person you become is a reflection of what you read and the people who you mix with • Buy three, hold two, sell one and pay down debt • One third land cost, one third build cost, one third your profit • Make the most of each hour • Avoid too many different trades working in the same space at the same time • Be on hand to do three vital tasks, answer questions, make decisions and ensure everyone has what they need to do their job

Follow the DavisHornsby Facebook page for more investor/ landlord musings and refurbishment tips.

CHAPTER 14 YOUR PROPERTY BUSINESS

How to run your property business could be an entirely separate book in itself. Revisiting the main points of my PUMA process is, in my opinion, one way to get off first base. Let's try to be brief.

A BUSINESS PLAN

You may recall my mentioning preparation of "G Incorporated", my business plan?

When you decide property is the business you intend to be in, it pays to have a business plan in which you state where your property journey is going, what actions you will take, how much money you need and what your critical success factors are. If "property" is going to be your career it will pay dividends to have a plan for your journey, from first investment to the time when you hang up your last Gantt chart, when you are debt free and can retire. Many working with property for themselves never truly retire. Why? I don't have all the answers. Maybe they are addicted to the buzz of property investment?

Let's recap on what we have been discussing together and apply it to your own property business.

- **P**lan your goals and plan how to achieve those goals.

- **U**nleash your energies towards those goals.
- **M**onitor how you and your business is progressing.
- **A**nalyse what you can do to get back on track and work towards your values and goals.

The first stage is to plan, based on your values and vision, encompassing those goals which you consider critical to your success. Know yourself and know your own values. Make sure your core values are preserved throughout your planning stage.

START WITH THE END IN MIND – VISION AND VALUES

Start with the end in mind. Make a conscious decision about where your business is going, why and what it will achieve.

- Are you going to become a multi- millionaire?
- Do you want to make sure you can have sufficient income to enjoy retirement and afford any necessary social and health care?
- Do you want to leave property for your dependents so that they can enjoy a kick start in life?

Among others, these are the sort of goals I see people aspiring to most often. There is no point embarking on a career investing in and managing property projects if you haven't thought what success is going to look like. You need a vision.

Vision alone is not enough. The best businesses have a strong sense of the values upon which the business is going to be built. Armed with a clear vision and sound values you can begin to apply the four stages you have learned about; plan first.

Remember that there are five steps in the Planning stage? Tread carefully. **T**asks, **R**esources, **E**stimates, **A**llowance for contingencies and **D**ependencies.

TASKS

In the same way you jotted down the tasks you needed to refurbish a property, jot down all the tasks you need to do to succeed in your property journey. You will typically need to:

- Determine the scope
- Carry out a SWOT and PEST analysis. We shall come to that.
- Get the necessary education.
- Determine location/s in which to work.
- Determine target annual profits (and cash flow).
- Set up appropriate insurances.
- Buy or acquire control of n properties.
- Refurbish properties.
- Develop key relationships.

Clearly there will be more detail in your business plan, but I trust you see the similarities to a refurbishing project. You will need to decide when you intend to do each of these tasks, who else might be involved, how much you can spend and where to place milestones or major check points.

SWOT THAT PEST

I mean undertake a SWOT (strengths, weaknesses, opportunities and threats) analysis and a PEST (political, environmental, socio-economical and technological) analysis.

Periodically consider what strengths there are in your business. Is it your own unique knowledge? Is it your team's loyalty and strong skills? Is your brand strong? Are you offering something no-one else has thought of?

Similarly consider what weaknesses there may be in your property business. Are you trying to do too much on your own? Are you maintaining your professional development and keeping up to date with legislation? Are you investing in the wrong areas or in the types of property for which there is no longer a strong demand?

Be open to spotting new opportunities, perhaps to diversify.

Think about what might threaten your success. Some who understand the "section 24" changes to UK tax regulations that have come into force, whereby you can no longer offset the interest on the money you have borrowed to fund your investments, see this as a threat to their bottom line. The key thing is to stay calm and work out what you can do about it.

National and local politics often have an impact on any business. Yours is no exception. UK rent caps, the expansion of the right to buy rules may (or may not) be on the horizon. Just be aware of what politics means to your journey.

The environment is very much in the news these days. From plastics to diesel, via disposal of building and decorating materials, we see many environmental factors that alter the way we invest and refurbish properties. How are you going to adapt to new environmental regulations, whilst continuing along your chosen path and protecting your profit / income?

As people live longer how are you ensuring your properties are refurbished to a standard that will attract these people? Is it in your interests and congruent with your values to offer more homes to people on benefits? The socio-economic climate is like shifting sand that you must keep your eye on in order to attain the vision you have of your own future.

The rate of change in technology has been almost unprecedented over the last decade, offering interesting opportunities for us. Think about the intelligent home, safety monitoring systems and how you communicate with your customers and your team. What new skills will you need? How cost effective is it to adopt various technological innovations?

I've only outlined a few points which emerge from these two powerful analyses. I hope you get the picture. It would be outside the scope of this guide to go into any depth here. You can always google PEST and SWOT analyses. However, what you should do is think about how each of those eight factors influence *how* you move towards your goals. Consider each one individually before looking for how combinations can help you move forward.

RESOURCES

In considering your whole property journey, think about the resources you will need. For the many individual refurbishment projects throughout your journey, each will need plumbers, electricians, painters, etc. For your property journey project / business you will need other resources including, among others, the following:

- A mentor – this is one of the most valuable resources
- Property business trainers (in all shapes and sizes)
- An accountant who understands the property business
- A tax advisor, who may be your accountant
- A legal advisor
- Estate and letting agents, some of which have dedicated staff who work with investors
- Someone with whom to share your successes
- Fellow property investors

This is not an exhaustive list, but I hope it gets you thinking.

ESTIMATES

In the same spirit as when you wrote your first estimates for each refurbishment project, write estimates of how many properties you need to control, how much each might cost in a particular area, how long each sub project is going to take and how many hours you will work each month / week/ day. No, the five day rule doesn't apply to each task in your property journey. I'd suggest three months might be in the right ball park region for timing sub projects in your business plan, each of which you'll plan and manage separately.

Against each sub project, budget whatever you consider to be the relevant funds. You can and should work up a cash flow forecast based on months or quarters throughout the duration of your big picture project. Many people plan and estimate for three or five years, undertake annual checks and then have a major review.

ALLOWANCES FOR CONTINGENCY

Treat this planning step in exactly the same way as you did for an individual refurbishment. Allow 10% to 20% contingency in terms of time and overall cost. Don't beat yourself up if it takes you six years instead of five years (that is 20% time contingency) to attain your overall goals. What more can I say about contingency? Make sure you include it.

DEPENDENCIES

Again, treat this step in the same way you did when we looked were looking at a refurbishment project. You can go back to the sort of questions I suggested in my mini four month project X. Ask yourself which tasks can or need to be undertaken at the same time as one another. Crucially ask yourself which things you need to do before you embark on something else. Clearly you will find it difficult to get off first base without knowing your business values or the scope of your business, so those two tasks must appear early on. I would suggest you will need to establish appropriate insurances before entering into any joint ventures with other investors, or acquiring another property.

Consider which things must have come to an end before you can do the next group of tasks. Is holding a celebration retirement / completion party dependent on your having reached a specific financial goal perhaps? Make sure you have business milestones at which you can reward yourself, but be honest with yourself and get the work done first.

UNLEASH YOUR EFFORTS

So far, so good. The second stage in the PUMA process is to unleash the workforce. In your business that is primarily you.

Once you have developed your business plan based on a sound analysis of the strengths, weaknesses, opportunities and threats to your business (not forgetting taking into account those external factors such as politics, economic climate, socio-economic landscape and technology) it is time to unleash yourself.

There is no need for you to remember everything in your five year plan because you have it written down. Your business plan is the road map for your personal success. You can use it to help persuade lenders to fund your projects; think about that.

JAWS will help you remember the steps within the UNLEASH stage. **J**ob / To Do Sheet, **A**uthorise the right people to get on with it, **W**elfare – yours, **S**tandard/s. Apply these to your overall property business.

JOB SHEET

Your "job sheet" might be a weekly or monthly "to do" list, taking in networking, reading, visiting accountants, checking your tax return (get the accountant to work it up), meeting with estate agents, attending auctions, meeting a direct vendor, checking insurances, viewing a property or tackling any number of other tasks. Remember actually to write down your "to do" list, including how much time you are spending on each task, who else is involved and what you intend to achieve, e.g. attending a one day auction is the task you plan to do, but acquiring a three bed house is what you intend to achieve.

AUTHORISE

Authorise the appropriate people to do the tasks. Do only the things you are good at and outsource the rest to someone who has the relevant skills.

Earlier I said "don't hover". The same principle applies to your business. Don't constantly fret about how things are going when you should be getting on with the tasks on your weekly list. Give yourself the space to focus on the tasks in hand, many of which will involve making use of your people skills and honing your influencing skills. Property is a people business as I've said before; perfecting the necessary skills takes time and is outside the scope of this guide.

Lean on the expertise of your accountant and your legal representative. When you are successful, others will challenge you in many ways; authorise your experts to deal with them.

Successful leaders and business people keep a mentor throughout their journey. Allow your mentor to make suggestions, query your decisions and advise; you remain responsible for making the final decisions.

WELFARE

We've talked about welfare of your workers on your project site (the individual property or block), but what about you? As you grow in your property business it is equally important to pay attention to yourself.

Get enough sleep. Eat healthily. Exercise regularly. You have never seen a fat puma avoiding hunting, but feasting exclusively on burgers and ice cream, have you? Let me know!

Look after the roof over your own head. Personally I would not use my main residence as security for a loan if I could possibly help it. In the early days of your investing/ refurbishing activities there are always going to be brokers who can tell you how to raise seed capital from your own home. Ask yourself how comfortable you are about doing that. Your mental welfare is vital to your success, so if you are uncomfortable risking your home, don't do it. You are the decision maker now.

Avoid worry and recognise when to take a break. You have read about the importance of relaxing at the appropriate time

STANDARDS

Don't let your standards slip. Telephoning vendors or agents in your pyjamas may be comfortable, but I'd suggest you will come across as more convincing if you dress and feel professional. Dress as you would to go to a JOB. Stand up to make 'phone calls; it helps focus your mind.

Keep an eye on the standard of what you achieve. If you planned to buy the three most run down houses in the best street you can afford, stick to that. Don't go buying something simply because you like it or it's "a good deal". It must serve your purpose and help you reach your goals.

For example if you plan to review your job list every Tuesday evening, don't leave it until the end of the week.

MONITOR

Monitoring your progress is the third stage in the PUMA process. In the context of your personal property journey, we have thought about the first two stages, viz. Planning and Unleashing the workforce. The difference between an individual property refurbishment and your journey is that we are now looking at your overall property journey; your business. It is indeed a business, whether you intended it to be or not.

DRAPE is, as no doubt you remember, what I use to remind me what I'm doing and what you are likely to be doing at this stage. DRAPE stands for. **D**elegation, **R**eporting, **A**ctuals, **P**roblems and **E**stimated end date.

DELEGATION

You'll be handing over some aspects of your business to professionals such as conveyancers, accountants and the like. Just as you made the distinction between delegation and abdication in your refurbishment projects, beware abdication of responsibility. Never just leave a conveyancer to complete all the stages in buying or selling a property; keep in touch and make sure they have all the documentation they need to do their work effectively.

Keeping an eye on how any conveyancing is progressing has been made much easier in recent years than it once was. Many solicitors, conveyancers and estate agents now use an on-line tracking system to store documents and record key points during the process. If you keep an eye on progress you'll know when to chase things up. You could consider delegating the task of monitoring conveyancing to someone else, but don't abdicate your responsibility.

It's your property journey, so you'll need to remain responsible for all aspects of that journey.

REPORTING

I can't emphasise enough the importance of getting regular reports from others to whom you have delegated certain tasks. Estate agents are a great example: if you asked them to find you a property with specific criteria, telephone once a week to see what progress they have made. Otherwise they tend to forget you, or worse, assume you are no longer looking.

You'll remember I have suggested sitting down with a cup of coffee, perhaps once a week and talking to yourself. Please, not out loud in a public place such as a coffee shop. Check what you have achieved against your "to do" list and allow yourself to feel good about it. Respect the fact you are only human, celebrate progress, keep others in the picture and focus on what successes you have already achieved and will achieve in the future.

Earlier in this guide I have gone into some detail about the various reporting flows, so I shall leave you to decide whether or not you need to go back and read that chapter again.

ACTUALS

Write down everything you have actually achieved each week. Make a note if something is taking up more time than planned and exactly by how much. If you are half way through a specific refurbishment project, take note so you can refer to it later.

Keep a record of actual time taken, actual costs of both materials and labour, as well as how much more money looks likely to be required to complete the tasks and how long each business task may take. You'll need actual costs of materials (receipts) and labour (invoices) in order to keep as evidence in case HMRC decide to investigate you. You can do the book keeping yourself or hire a professional to do the book keeping, accounts and tax returns, all from the actual records you keep.

Be organised. Not only do I have a separate file / folder for each property project, but I also have several for the overall business. Details of those items pertinent to the overall business are held in there. What am I talking about? I'm talking about things such as liability and professional indemnity insurances, training, physical equipment inventory (e.g. PC, laser measure, tools) and transport (car perhaps). Keeping actual receipts is essential to the success of your business; once filed away properly you need not fret about what you have done with them.

Consider those intangible tasks too, such as building relationships, and see how they are going. Spot what actual evidence there is for measuring your how well you have performed. If you have good testimonials from 90% of your tenants, I'd suggest that is an actual measureable achievement. Keep the evidence.

PROBLEMS

When we talked about problems on a specific refurbishment project, we included things like people, health and safety and money. Spot any problems in your business before they become a crisis.

Periodically, look at yourself. Relationships must be maintained; treat them like a car and have routine maintenance / health checks. Are you really getting enough quality sleep? There is little point in making a pile of money if you end up too tired to pay attention to those you love and care about.

Many health and safety issues in your business, along with people challenges, can be addressed by taking a little time out to relax, talk or top up your personal development with reading or training. Generally, I plan to take about a week out each year to go and get my education topped up. Ask yourself if you are getting the right degree of appropriate training. When did you last enjoy a meal with friends and family or take a holiday?

Money is of course a common cause of problems in many a business. No matter how well you planned your cash flow and eventual wealth growth, things can and do go wrong sometimes. Monitor your finances regularly. Check your actual bank balances, loan arrangements and credit cards.

ESTIMATED END DATE - RETIREMENT

Don't leave it five years to monitor the situation! Check in with yourself, perhaps quarterly. Ask yourself how much longer you will need to reach your interim goals. Monitoring in this way will enable you to maintain control. Determine when you will reach the next milestone in your business plan. Estimate your end date for tasks up to the next milestone. If it looks like a challenge make a note to yourself.

Unless you know where you are going, how you are going to get there and when you will arrive, may I suggest you are unlikely to arrive in time to enjoy the fruits of your labours.

ANALYSE

Be an AVID analyser. As you have learned before, this is the fourth and final stage of the puma project process. It is time to look at your observations, analyse the situation realistically and make business decisions. You recall that AVID stands for **A**ctuals v Plan, **V**ariances, **I**ndicators and **D**ecisions.

ACTUALS v PLAN and VARIANCES

Compare your finances against your business cash flow forecast. See if you are running out of funds or getting into unnecessary debt. Compare what lenders actually lent you to the sums you had believed they would.

Compare what you have actually achieved against the business work plan, especially the key milestones. If you had intended to acquire 3 properties a month, check in with yourself and see how many you have actually secured and how many remain in the pipeline.

Exactly as you did for an individual project, calculate the differences arising from your comparison of actuals against plan. You now know the specific degree of variance from your business plan and can see how far behind or ahead you are. You can assess how much contingency you have used up.

INDICATORS

As well as the hard facts you have just considered there may be indicators that something is not quite right with your business. You will, undoubtedly, be concerned about what your business is doing for you, your friends and family.

Are you chasing your own tail trying to do too much too soon? Are you enjoying the journey or are you allowing yourself to become stressed? Are you attempting to do those things for which you are not really trained, yet?

Are you over spending or letting credit card debt build up? Are your loan repayments being made on time, every time?

Is your only topic of conversation your property journey? Are you in danger of appearing obsessive?

Keep a look out for challenges on the horizon before they harm your business or your relationships.

DECISIONS

The saying *"if it's going to be it's up to me"*, is so true when managing your personal property journey. Once you have analysed your situation, based on actual evidence, you are free to decide what to do. Keep questioning your progress, making decisions and reworking your business plan If necessary and be prepared to go around the cycle as many times as it takes.

It is OK to take a day off, relax or go out for the day, ending with a nice dinner with your significant other. It is fine to spend a few hours chatting over topics outside your business. It is up to you to make a conscious decision regarding what you do to mend and maintain relationships.

Your health and welfare are largely, but not entirely, in your own hands. Making sensible decisions about sleep, food and exercise can keep you firing on all cylinders, thus helping you to reach your goals for property success. Never neglect your health. Make decisions about your health on a timely basis, making many small adjustments, before something becomes a crisis. In honour of the memory of Stephen Hawking, I have to point out that health issues need not stop you from achieving your property goals. Look at what he achieved. So, no excuses. Make the best decisions for your life and business that you can.

Never put off making decisions about money. Aim to keep a float in each bank account and make sure you do not go below that. Aim to pay off credit card balances at the end of the month. Stickers on your fridge and bathroom mirror reading "begrudge the banks interest" are a powerful motivator; my other half and I have used this tactic in the past. If your loan repayments are proving irksome, deal with the situation promptly. This is both important and urgent. Seek advice from your accountant, a debt agency or your bank if you are finding it too difficult to make the decisions yourself.

Seeking help could be the best decision you make.

FINALLY

As we have worked through this guide you will have developed a good basic understanding of how to manage a residential property refurbishment project, using the PUMA as an aide memoire. You've also given some thought to proactively managing your own property journey. I look forward to hearing about your success.

As you have seen glimpses of how I used my past experiences and overcame disadvantage and hurdles, you will have learned from my mistakes and you will have probably changed. You are now well equipped to handle your property challenges in a systematic way with confidence.

I know you can manage both your next project and yourself.

Value yourself and allow yourself time to smell the roses.

****

FURTHER SOURCES OF INFORMATION

REGULAR PROPERTY UPDATES

Websites, blogs and Forums – Here are just a few.

www.propertytribes.com

www.propertyhub.net

www.propertyforum.com

www.landlordzone.co.uk

www.property118.com

www.lnpg.co.uk

www.landlords.org.uk

www.ons.gov.uk

www.hse.gov.uk

www.davishornsby.co.uk

READING

Besides reading the newspapers regularly to spot trends and opportunities emerging, you can benefit hugely from reading several different types of material, be it in book form, on your Kindle, or listening to audio books and podcasts whilst driving (that is my favourite lazy girl way of learning). I love real books, but do find listening to property training, as I'm driving along, both time efficient and relaxing. Whichever form it takes, I feel strongly that to become a rounded property investor/ landlord/ project manager, reading daily is "a must". My reading focus, and I suggest it could be yours too, includes:

- Keeping up to date with ever changing legislation (journals and the internet)
- People skills (books and on-line training)
- Your own mental attitude and self-esteem (books)
- Personal development (books)
- Feedback from tenants and property agents (emails)
- Finance (newspapers and online forums)
- Property investment trends (online forums, online property sales sites, Office of National Statistics and journals)

MAGAZINES

Homebuilding and Renovating

Your Property Network

Property Investor News

Property Week

Real Homes

Residential Property Investor

UK Landlord (for NLA members)

BOOKS

Grow Rich With Peace of Mind - Napoleon Hill
(ISBN 0-449-21525-3)

The Age of Unreason: New Thinking For A New World -
Charles Handy (ISBN: 9780099548317)

Rhinoceros Success - Scott Alexander (ISBN: 0-937382-00-0)

Action Centred Leadership - John Adair (ISBN 0-566-02143-9)

The Time Trap: How to Get More Done in Less Time -
R.Alec Mackenzie (ISBN 0-07-044650-4)

The One minute Manager: Increase Productivity, Profits, and Your Own Prosperity - Kenneth Blanchard, PhD and Spencer John, M.D. (ISBN 0-688-01429-1)

Rich Dad Poor Dad: What The Rich Teach Their Kids About Money That The Poor and Middle Class Do Not! - Robert Kiyosaki (ISBN 978-1-61268-000-2)

Feel the Fear and Do It Anyway - Susan Jeffers
(ISBN 978-0091907075)

The 7 Habits of Highly Effective People - Dr.Stephen R Covey
(ISBN 978-8934901501)

The Rich Rules: Steps to Wealth and Happiness - Kevin Green
(ISBN 0993169309, 9780993169304)

****

Printed in Great Britain
by Amazon

33578976R00115